The Political Integration of Women

The Political Integration of Women:

ROLES, SOCIALIZATION, AND POLITICS

Virginia Sapiro

UNIVERSITY OF ILLINOIS PRESS

Urbana and Chicago

To Rose M. Michaels

1898-1980

Illini Books edition, 1984

©1983 by the Board of Trustees of the University of Illinois
Manufactured in the United States of America
P   4   3

This book is printed on acid-free paper.

Library of Congress Cataloging in Publication Data

Sapiro, Virginia.
  The political integration of women.

  Bibliography: p.
  Includes index.
  1. Women in politics—United States.
  2. Political socialization—United States.
  3. Sex role—United States. I. Title.
  HQ1236.S27   306′.2   82-2672
  ISBN 0-252-01141-4   AACR2

Acknowledgments

Feminist writers have a habit of reaching far back into their child-hoods in their prefaces in order to expose the sources of their development as feminists. I have tried to suppress that urge, and therefore I will not thank the stage manager of the Romper Room television show of 1955 who gave some unknown little boy and me our first taste of sex discrimination when he forced us to exchange toys because the ones we were playing with were gender inappro-priate. I also won't thank the little boy for making the only moral response: he joined me in a terrific temper tantrum that forced the stage manager to retreat soundly defeated.

This book was conceived at the University of Michigan, and numerous people there between 1972 and 1976 provided support and assistance that cannot be repaid. The participants in the Women's Caucus in the Department of Political Science served not only as an essential support group, but also helped give me my first opportunity to teach a course on women and politics. Teaching such courses is how most of the women in this field learned the material. Numerous friends, office partners, faculty, and staff at the Center for Political Studies helped, in their various ways, to keep me sane. I owe particular debts to Barbara Farah and Stan Seltzer. My special affection to Graham Wilson for being there in the final stages.

This book bears the marks of criticism and suggestions offered by Mel Croan, Murray Edelman, Barbara Hinckley, Kent Jennings, Dick Merelman, Warren Miller, and Ben Page. I thank them all for their personal and intellectual gifts. I should also point out that their role was in improving the manuscript; any remaining errors are mine, as are the values expressed and embedded here.

My greatest appreciation goes to Kent Jennings, who has served as mentor, employer, therapist, and friend. Without him this book could not exist. He provided access to an intriguing set of data, supervised the first birth of the manuscript (its previous incarnation), and has remained an important teacher and critic.

This book is dedicated to my grandmother, Rose M. Michaels. She gave me the gift of reading and writing and continues to teach me how to think and feel. This book is hers.

V.S.

Contents

List of Tables

CHAPTER 1

Introduction

Girls! although I am a woman,
I always try to appear human.[1]

The first full length work of the first American novelist, Charles
Brockden Brown, is a feminist utopian fiction. Published in 1797
under the title *Alcuin: A Dialogue*, it presents Brown's Wollstone-
craft-inspired observations of women in the polity in the form of
a conversation between Alcuin and his hostess, Mrs. Carter, during
successive evening gatherings at her home.[2] Alcuin, socially inept
and at a loss for topics of polite conversation, asks Mrs. Carter,
"Pray, Madame, are you a Federalist?" Mrs. Carter, apparently inno-
cently, responds that she cannot be a Federalist because she is a
woman, and politics is not the place for women. We soon find Mrs.
Carter teasing poor Alcuin along, allowing him to voice objections
to her feminine modesty. By the end of the conversation her line
has changed:

When I see myself, in my relation to my society, regarded
merely as a beast, or an insect; passed over, in the distribution
of public duties, as absolutely nothing, by those who disdain
to assign the least apology for their injustice — what though politicians say I am nothing, it is impossible I should assent to their
opinion, as long as I am conscious of willing and moving. If
they generously admit me into the class of existence, but affirm
that I exist for no purpose but the convenience of the more
dignified sex; that I am not to be entrusted with the government of myself; that to foresee, to deliberate and decide, belongs
to others, while all my duties resolve themselves into this pre-
cept, "listen and obey"; it is not for me to smile at this tyranny,
or receive, as my gospel, a code built upon such atrocious
maxims. No, I am no federalist.[3]

In either case the woman feels herself marginal to the world of politics, but the implications of her explanations differ vastly.

The "first" Mrs. Carter is devoid of any feminist consciousness. She is the dutiful hostess, managing the private sphere of social relations, who sticks to her home and accepts the dictum that politics is man's business. Such a woman may be content to leave the governing to others, to her father, husband, or brother to speak for her. Despite the fact that government affects her as much as it affects anyone, and restricts her more, she would take no part in determining how it will affect her. She is, perhaps, a loyal subject, but she is no citizen.

The "second" Mrs. Carter has no more political power than the first, and she is also marginal to politics. But unlike the first, she has the political consciousness of a feminist. She does not proudly declare her marginality: she understands it to be an arbitrary and unjust rule of society that binds her simply because she is a woman. Her consciousness of her marginality is the source of her discontent. She denies being a Federalist not because politics is irrelevant to her, but because the Federalists have rejected her (albeit through inaction) as irrelevant to them.

Contemporary studies of women and politics reveal the existence of women like "both" Mrs. Carters today. There are women who renounce interest or at least explain their lack of interest in politics on grounds of their womanhood or femininity. There are also increasing numbers of women who, as part of the women's movement, are taking the political system to task for rejecting or, at best, ignoring them. There are many other ways in which we can see gender shaping both women's political roles and the ways in which the public and political leaders interpret women's relationship to the political system. Some women neither withdraw from politics nor express discontent, but feel that women are capable of unique (relative to men) contributions in areas of politics that coincide with traditional stereotypes of femininity. Many women, of course, fail to notice the ways in which gender affects their own political roles. In a male-dominated political system, however, it would be difficult to locate women whose gender is completely irrelevant to their political lives, particularly because of the stereotypes through which women are viewed. One might argue, for example, that women who hold political offices have transcended or broken through the barriers of gender stratification. Research on women shows, to the contrary, that even when a female officeholder does not view herself as a representative of her gender, she is as likely as not to be viewed by others as a *woman* politician rather than, simply, as a politician.[4]

Unfortunately, until recently social scientists (and especially political scientists) have done little to advance our understanding of gender stratification and differentiation. Academic circles are by no means immune to the social forces that shape the rest of society. Before the advent of the women's movement, for example, the official and most prestigious journal of the American Political Science Association contained, between 1906 and 1973, two articles that focused on women's political roles.[5] The sixty-eighth volume of that quarterly journal contained the third, a review article.[6] Between 1974 and 1981 the number more than doubled.[7] Before 1970 there were virtually no courses on women and politics,[8] and courses and books on politics were not very likely to include the merest mention of women.

The lack of attention to women cannot be attributed solely to the relative paucity of female political scientists. In fact, statistics on employment and education show that the proportion of women found among academics, including social scientists, was about the same in the 1930s as it was in 1970.[9] The problem is more a normative and political one.[10] Women do not appear in political life as much as men do in part because they are not valued and encouraged in politics as much as men are; they do not "fit" into politics as comfortably. Women and women's issues do not appear in political research and teaching as much as do men and the issues they consider important in part because they are not valued as much as men are; they do not "fit" into the concerns of political science as comfortably. Therefore the majority of people working on the study of women or the links between gender and politics have had to do so without the respect of the bulk of their colleagues and often against the advice of their friends and associates, not to mention those who control hiring, firing, and purse-strings. Those who have succeeded have lept hurdles few men encounter.

Research on gender and politics involves the same difficulties as does doing research on any problem. There are the same brilliant flashes in the middle of the night that are revealed as mundane when the sun rises. Women's studies scholars also must clarify our concepts, refine theory, solve methodological problems, face writers' blocks, and cope with the perils of finding an "outlet." But the field of women's studies presents added burdens to the already tortured mind of the researchers. Beside the problems mentioned above, two others bear direct relevance to the process of writing — and reading — this book.

The first, which stems from the lack of attention to women within the dominant concerns of political science, is what we might call the "literature review" problem. Where there are courses or even case studies within courses there is a "literature," a set of well-known works and generally recognized concepts, concerns, and arguments to which one might refer for assistance, enlightenment, and warning. In fact, readers expect to see certain familiar names among the footnotes, and they expect not to see too many unfamiliar ones. In contrast, women's studies scholars are inventing their literature now. This does not mean that worthwhile articles and books did not exist until the last few years. To the contrary, one could fill library shelves with the sometimes brilliant works of those who have sought to understand gender differentiation and stratification in the past.[11] But these works have been erased in the collective consciousness of academics because the subject matter was not deemed important. Our footnotes, therefore, do not necessarily contain the familiar names that prove membership in the ongoing community of scholars. They do contain many names that are not recognized (in both senses of the word) by the mainstream of our fields.[12] This problem is exacerbated by the interdisciplinary nature of most studies of women. People within one discipline often seem uncomfortable in the company of names from another.

A second problem has to do with the audience for books on women. Much of the writing on women and politics is designed for three audiences which differ in background, needs, and expectations. The field of women's studies within the study of politics is relatively small, and its members are hungry for any new insights. Those with a commitment to teaching and research in this area do not have the luxury of designing their work specifically for either students on the one hand or advanced researchers on the other, as is true in most areas. At the date of this writing, for example, there is no basic, comprehensive text on women and politics, although some are in progress. It is not easy to produce a book that can be used to advantage by students, advanced scholars working in the field, and advanced scholars new to the specific field. That, however, is the likely composition of the audience for any book on women and politics.

Another segment of the audience presents even greater problems, largely because it is notable by its absence. As is the case in any field, we do not address ourselves only to those who are predominantly interested in our substantive concerns. If information on women and politics is to be integrated into the general knowledge of our disciplines, people outside women's studies must become familiar with our work. Moreover, many works on women and politics, and certainly this one, are not designed solely to add to knowledge about women. Our specific foci also serve as vehicles for adding to knowledge about a variety of political concerns and processes. Many women's studies scholars have probably felt the urge to title their articles something like, "Don't Stop Reading This Just Because It's about Women." In addition, the assumption that women's studies research is polemical or politicized (as opposed to scholarly and objective) appears to distort the reading ability of many non–women's studies readers. Reviews of books on women continue, upon occasion, to compliment the author for not being "shrill" or "polemical" because that is still the expectation. It sometimes appears that female academics are expected to fill one of two models. They may be silent about themselves and their problems and be regarded as scholarly or they may focus on gender stratification and be regarded as polemical and political. The underlying problems of the study of women and politics, then, are very closely related to the underlying problems of women in politics, the issue to which we turn next.

Marginality and Integration

In 1951, sociologist Helen Hacker tried to understand women's place in society by applying the concepts of intergroup relations to the case of gender.[13] Hacker argued that the concept of marginality could be especially helpful to students of gender differentiation and stratification. "Marginality" is defined as the state in which one "lives in two different worlds simultaneously," where one "is a participant in two cultural systems, one of which is, by prevailing stand-

ards, regarded as superior to the other."[14] Hacker, like Mirra Komarovsky before her, noticed that women's lives were being dominated
increasingly by cultural contradictions.[15] Women, especially members of the growing group who were entering universities and the
job market, were judged and were judging themselves by two different, and contradictory, standards at once. One was the standard
of femininity, by which one must be nurturant, passive, emotional,
home-oriented, and subordinate to men. The other standard was
that of the "modern role," by which one is judged on the principles
of rationality, striving, and achievement in the open market.

The concept of marginality focuses our attention on the nexus
of culture and personality. The cultural norms, institutionalized in
human organization and social procedures, are translated at the individual level as personality characteristics, goals, and personal and
interpersonal standards of evaluation. As Komarovsky points out,
marginality creates a situation in which "the goals set out by each
role are mutually exclusive, and the fundamental personality traits
each evokes are at points diametrically opposed, so that what are
assets for one become liabilities for the other, and the full realiza-
tion of one role threatens defeat in the other."[16]

Komarovsky, Hacker, and others since then have focused on role
conflict within the condition of marginality, the effects on women's
personalities, and the strategies women use to cope with such conflict. Conflict-induced anxiety as well as other psychological and
physiological problems have been well documented.[17] Women are
increasingly attempting to satisfy both standards, thus doubling their
work. In the end, however, no amount of compartmentalization
can erase the problem of marginality. As Hacker argued over three
decades ago, because of "interiorized cultural notions of feminine
inferiority in certain fields, . . . even the most self-confident or most
defensive woman may be filled with doubt as to whether she can
do productive work."[18]

As Marianne Githens and Jewel Prestage point out, the concept
of marginality is well suited to analysis of women's relations to the
political world.[19] In recent years many scholars have traced the
growing bifurcation of the public domain of politics and the private domain, especially of the family.[20] The public-private split is
of critical importance in the history of gender roles and relations.
Women have remained embedded in the private world; the stand-

ards of femininity are essentially private values. Participants in the political world are judged on very different grounds. Women in politics, therefore, are evaluated by two different standards: first, the standard of femininity, and second, the standards of politics, nonfeminine and superior to the feminine. It is expected that the actions of women in politics are derived from their central private concerns of wifehood, motherhood, and homemaking, although in the public world of politics these concerns are seen as peculiar and, to a large degree, inappropriate. Political philosophers tell us that man is by nature political; they also tell us that woman by nature is not.[21] Thus, by dint of their marginality, women in politics have two choices. They may view themselves and act in the political world according to the prevailing standards of politics and be seen as unfeminine, or they may view themselves and act in politics according to the standards of femininity and be seen at best as peculiarities.

The opposite of marginality is integration. If the worlds of womanhood and politics were integrated, there would be nothing peculiar about women's involvement in politics, or politics' involvement in what are now labeled as "women's issues." (What would a "woman's issue" be if the private world of the family and the public world of politics were not so split from each other or if men and women shared equally in both family and political concerns?) Women now have political rights and they do participate in politics, but they are not yet fully integrated into the political world.

When we focus on political integration we are really asking questions about the quality of women's membership in a political community; we are examining the degree to which women are full citizens. Citizenship connotes more than nationality. Citizenship entails the liberty, even the responsibility, to share in the governance and political life of a community. Many people have argued that even if women do not have full roles in the political sphere, they live full and important lives in the private sphere of the family, where women's power lies. Public activity, the argument continues, is therefore not as important to women as it is to men. This analysis flies in the face of the democratic revolutions, reforms, and theories of the last few centuries. Participation in the governance of one's community is participation in the governance of oneself. Those who are governed but do not govern are not citizens but subjects. If women's private roles impede their political opportunity, those roles, and the policies that maintain them, ultimately impede control over their lives. When we ask about political integration of women we are asking about the roles women play within the political world, but also the relative role politics plays in women's lives. Without power in the political world, in fact, women cannot have a full measure of power in private life — not, at least, as long as government is in part responsible for regulating fertility, sexuality, divisions of labor and property in the family, and the conditions under which one forms or dismantles the family.

This book, then, does not seek to answer Henry Higgins's question, "Why can't a woman be more like a man?" It seeks, rather, to reveal the connections between women's private roles and their political roles, to find out the ways in which women's private roles shape the form and substance of mass political behavior and attitudes. This is not a comparative study of women and men; that is a separate question and would make a different book. It is a study of the connections between different parts of women's lives. It is, in large part, a study of political development, of the processes by which women as a group and women as individuals are being transformed — and, indeed, are transforming themselves — into citizen members of the political community.

The Itinerary

The task of this book is to explore through theoretical and historical discussion and empirical analysis the relationship between women's private roles and socialization, on the one hand, and their integration into politics on the other. We will focus on the development of women both as individuals and as a group into citizens and political persons. Chapters 2 and 3 rely primarily on historical sources and socialization theory and prior research to frame the argument and generate hypotheses about women's development. The second part of the book, Chapters 4 through 7, tests these hypotheses using as its data base the Michigan Socialization Panel Study, a survey which will be described in more detail later. Finally, the Conclusion outlines the significance of this study for public policy and feminist theory.

Although this book concentrates primarily on present day political roles, we begin with a socio-historical analysis of female integration into politics in Chapter 2. If political integration must be measured by more than reference to laws and policies that allow women to participate in politics, we need a framework within which to understand how a social group (and its members) develops new relationships with the political system. It is also not enough simply to chart, for example, voter turnout of women since 1920. Trying to understand the relationship of women to political culture in this manner would cast little more light than would trying to understand Soviet political culture by beginning with 1917. Rather, we shall treat the policies that sanction women's participation in politics as changes in formal opportunities, and focus on underlying norms and roles within a historical context.

Large-scale socio-historical forces do not in and of themselves account for the ways in which individuals participate in their political cultures. Chapter 3 develops further the analytical framework for this study by looking to the process of political socialization for the connections between political culture and development on the one hand and individual role assumption on the other. Many psychologists and sociologists (and fewer political scientists) have looked to socialization for the key to women's role behavior; for this reason some of the information in this chapter will be new only to those with little background in women's studies. These prior studies document quite clearly the ways in which the environment of children is designed to create very different male and female political subcultures. What is less well documented is the *effect* of the agents of socialization. Recent evidence has shown little differentiation in the political attitudes and behavior of children. This observation has led some to claim that the problem of political stratification by gender is being solved of its own accord. Feminists who emphasize socialization as both the source of and the solution to women's problems also simplify the situation. Recent studies show that male and female political roles become increasingly differentiated in the early stages of adulthood. Chapter 3 therefore emphasizes the timing of political learning, and the differences and connections between the learning of norms and enactment of those norms. It underscores the role of private institutions such as the family not simply as agents of political socialization for children but, perhaps more powerfully, for adults.

Armed with analyses of women's association with the political world on both the societal and the individual level, we turn in Chapter 4 to empirical investigation of the relationship between women's private and political roles. That chapter introduces the data that are used in the empirical portion of this study (Chapters 4-7) and outlines and explains the research design. The data are drawn from a survey of women in their twenties in 1973, which allows us to focus on gender roles and politics in one of the first generations of women to come of age in the era following the birth of the Women's Liberation Movement. The findings of this study are therefore not generalizable to all adults currently in the American political system; rather, it should provide insights into patterns developing among the generations of "new women."

Chapters 5 through 7 focus on the relationship of gender roles to different aspects of political involvement including, successively, political orientations, political communication and participation, and issue orientations. The goal of these chapters is a refinement of the conceptual and empirical connections drawn between private and public roles within one cultural system. How, for example, is participation in the institution of marriage or motherhood affecting women today?

In the Conclusion we return to the political system level of analysis by focusing especially on public policies that affect women's private roles and thereby, albeit indirectly, their roles in politics. If, for example, traditional divisions of labor within the home help to constrain women's political participation, policies that help to maintain such divisions of labor must be seen as in part responsible for the political marginality of women. Seen in this light we can argue that public policy that is intended to affect what are usually regarded as private affairs in fact also serves to shape the nature of citizenship and public affairs. Analysis of women and politics shows, perhaps better than does any other case, the profoundly interlocked character of the two domains people often falsely assume and vainly wish to be distinct. In the end, therefore, this book is not "just" about women, although common opinion to the contrary, that would be important enough. It is about how our private and public roles shape, maintain, and change each other.

NOTES

1. Stevie Smith, cited in Viola Klein, *The Feminine Character: A History of an Ideology* (Urbana: University of Illinois Press, 1972), p. 179.

2. Charles Brockden Brown, *Alcuin: A Dialogue* (New York: Grossman Publishers, 1970).
3. *Ibid.*, p. 30.
4. Jeane Kirkpatrick, *Political Woman* (New York: Basic, 1974); Irene Diamond, *Sex Roles in the State House* (New Haven: Yale University Press, 1977); Susan Carroll, "Women Candidates and Support for Women's Issues: Closet Feminists," paper presented to the Annual Meeting of the Midwest Political Science Association, Chicago, 1979.
5. Alzada Comstock, "Women Members of European Parliaments," *American Political Science Review* 20 (1926), 379-83; Marguerite Fisher and Betty Whitehead, "Women's Participation in National Party Nominating Conventions, 1892-1941," *American Political Science Review* 38 (Oct., 1944), 395-403.
6. Wilma Rule Krauss, "Political Implications of Gender Roles: A Review of the Literature," *American Political Science Review* 68 (Dec., 1974), 1706-23.
7. Melissa A. Butler, "Early Liberal Roots of Feminism: John Locke and His Attack on Patriarchy," *American Political Science Review* 72 (Mar., 1978), 135-50; Diane L. Fowlkes, Jerry Perkins, and Sue Tolleson Rinehart, "Gender Roles and Party Roles," *American Political Science Review* 73 (Sept., 1979), 772-80; Jerry Perkins and Diane L. Fowlkes, "Opinion Representation versus Social Representation; Or, Why Women Can't Run as Women and Win," *American Political Science Review* 74 (Mar., 1980), 92-103; Virginia Sapiro, "When Are Interests Interesting? The Problem of Political Representation of Women," *American Political Science Review* 75 (Sept., 1981), 701-16.
8. There were some, apparently. The 1914-15 bulletin of the University of Wisconsin–Madison lists a course in the Political Science Department entitled, "The Legal and Political Status of Women."
9. Barbara Deckard Sinclair, *The Women's Movement* (New York: Harper and Row, 1979).
10. For political analyses of the growth of women's studies within political science see Jean Bethke Elshtain, "Methodological Sophistication and Conceptual Confusion: A Critique of Mainstream Political Science," in Julia Sherman and Evelyn Beck, eds., *The Prism of Sex: Essays in the Sociology of Knowledge* (Madison: University of Wisconsin Press, 1979), pp. 229-52, and Virginia Sapiro, "Women's Studies and Political Conflict," in Sherman and Beck, *The Prism of Sex*, pp. 253-66.
11. This is not the place to attempt to provide a roll of "great women." Their names are scattered throughout works on women.
12. Of the names that are recognizable to non–women's studies scholars, many of the works are not, or at least not commonly, read. The books or chapters on women written by the likes of Tocqueville or J. S. Mill tend to be regarded as minor works, not worthy of attention.
13. Helen Hacker, "Women as a Minority Group," *Social Forces* 30 (Oct., 1951), 60-69.
14. Klein, *The Feminine Character*, pp. 171-72.

15. Mirra Komarovsky, "Cultural Contradictions and Sex Roles," *American Journal of Sociology* 52 (Nov., 1946), 184-89.
16. *Ibid.*, p. 184.
17. On role conflict see Judith Bardwick, *Psychology of Women: A Study of Bio-Cultural Conflicts* (New York: Harper and Row, 1971).
18. Hacker, "Women as a Minority Group," p. 69.
19. Marianne Githens and Jewel Prestage, "Introduction," in M. Githens and J. Prestage, eds., *A Portrait of Marginality: The Political Behavior of American Women* (New York: Longman, 1977), pp. 3-10.
20. For example, Richard Sennett, *The Fall of Public Man: On the Social Psychology of Capitalism* (New York: Random House, 1976); Jean Bethke Elshtain, "Moral Woman and Immoral Man: A Consideration of the Public-Private Split and Its Political Ramifications," *Politics and Society* 4 (Winter, 1974), 453-74; Robert Paul Wolff, "There's Nobody Here But Us Persons," in Carol Gould and Marx Wartofsky, eds., *Women and Philosophy* (New York: G.P. Putnam's Sons, 1976), pp. 128-44.
21. For discussions of women in the history of political philosophy, see especially Susan Okin, *Women in Western Political Thought* (Princeton: Princeton University Press, 1979) and Jean Bethke Elshtain, *Public Man, Private Woman: Women in Social and Political Thought* (Princeton: Princeton University Press, 1981).

CHAPTER 2

Women and Politics

Politics and women. For most people at most times these two words
have harmonized neither on paper nor in the mind. They are
cacophonous words, contradictory terms. Together they call up
amusing pictures, Nast-like images of cigar-smoking women in crino-
lines. Just as often, this vision is a nightmare: "The conclusive objection to the political franchise of women is, that it would weaken
and finally break up and destroy the Christian family. Extend now
to women suffrage . . . and what remains of family union will soon
be dissolved. The wife may espouse one political party and the husband another, and it may well happen that the husband and wife
may be rival candidates for the same office."[1] Increasing involvement of women in political life has been blamed for the spread of
a wide range of "social evils" at various times: dissolution of the
family and society itself, communism, anarchy, juvenile delin-
quency, adultery, and worst of all, the loss of those exquisite feminine charms that make life so pleasant and intriguing. For a long
time it was virtually impossible to view women's involvement in
politics in a "normal" way; if women were considered an integral
part of the political system, and if they were thought to have the
same political roles and functions as their male counterparts, the
situation was atypical or extraordinary, and therefore not normal.

Through most of history, political participation was restricted
by and large to the elite in any case: the monarchs and advisors
and, in varying degrees, the aristocracy. Gender differentiation in
politics became clearer as increasing options for political involvement
were granted to (or appropriated by) the common person. As rights

were usually granted to men first. In England
es women could not be granted many political
arried women, the law did not even recognize
ersons." In his 1765 *Commentaries*, Sir William
e interpretation of the law that has been an
ts since: "By marriage, the husband and wife
w; that is, the very being or legal existence of
the women is suspended during the marriage, or at least in incorporated and consolidated into that of the husband; under whose
wing, protection, and *cover*, she performs everything."[2] This sentiment had overwhelming influence in both England and the United
States. It was only in the 1840s that married women in the United
States were granted the right to own property. Before then, they
were considered part of their husband's "chattel," and property cannot own property.

In all matters the wife was incorporated into the husband; in political matters he was her representative or, as Paul has said centuries
earlier, her head. While many people to this day define the family
as the basic unit of society, without considering the status and rights
of women one cannot grasp the full extent to which this has been
true. Marx wrote over a century ago that the first division of labor
the first division of "capitalist" from "proletarian" could be found
in the male-female relationship in the family. The first division of
the political labor of representation may also be found in this relationship. Representation originally did not refer to the representation of districts of individuals. Rather, members of legislatures represented districts of families. In a reduction of political affairs to
its smallest unit, we find that the family was one such unit; each
of these units had an interest determined by the station or occupation of the head of the household. (This norm is still accepted; both
official and unofficial records still list the man in the house, if there
is a man in the house, as the "head of household.") In political matters the family was and still is to some degree a brokerage; it was
the husband's duty to express the interests of his family — including
that of the adult female member — when he cast his vote for a representative of the district in which he resided. When women began
to agitate for the vote they agitated for the right to represent themselves. Antisuffragists argued that women did not need the vote
because they were already represented by their husbands. The

woman who did not feel adequately represented by her husband was displaying her inadequacy as a wife.

The liberal challenge to the aristocracy in the late eighteenth and early nineteenth centuries had a lasting impact on conceptions of the rights and duties of women. Throughout the eighteenth century and into the nineteenth, concern with individualism in not only economic but also in political terms gained increasing influence. Just as middle-class men no longer accepted political restrictions that were due to a lack of inherited wealth and title, some women would no longer accept restrictions that were due to lack of certain inherited physical organs. As the liberal democratic ideas gained sway, women found the restrictions placed on them less palatable.

The protests that were part of the early agitation ranged from the political essays of Mary Wollstonecraft or Margaret Fuller to the almost happenstance letters of Abigail Adams.[3] Although the work and writing of the early feminists documents the progress and rationale of changes in the political status of women, Adams's letters to her husband, John, and her friend the historian Mercy Otis Warren are very telling with regard to the degree to which women began to chafe under the political restrictions placed on them.[4] Adams was no extraordinary woman; she was not a political activist or thinker. She was an obviously bright woman who had to cope as so many others did while her husband was away for lengthy periods of time, particularly during the revolution. She has a place in history only because of her marriage to the second president of the United States.

The famous letter Abigail Adams wrote to her husband in 1776 declaring that women were "determined to foment a rebellion" if not granted extended rights under the new government was written at least in part in jest, as we can see from her later letter to Warren. When John responded with a solicitous letter telling his wife in effect that women's hands already rocked the cradle and thus ruled the world Abigail became angry. She became part of a developing undercurrent of discontent among women and men. Although such people were not mobilized into action until many years later, increasing numbers of Americans probably nodded their heads in agreement when they read words such as the following, which appeared anonymously in a 1791 newspaper:

What we read, in days of yore,
   the woman's occupation,
Was to direct the wheel and loom,
   Not to direct the nation.
This narrow minded policy
   by us hath met detection;
While woman's bound, man can't be free,
   nor have a fair election.[5]

Women's legal rights and their opportunities expanded slowly through the nineteenth and early twentieth centuries. The Married Women's Property Acts in the 1840s were the first major assaults on the legal edifice that imprisoned women. At the same time the women's colleges now known as the Seven Sisters began to open, and Oberlin became the first college to enroll both men and women. Once women could own their own property and receive an education, the next target was the world of employment. Through the nineteenth century and into the twentieth women began to trickle and then to rush into occupations previously closed to members of their sex. By 1930, for example, the proportion of doctors, lawyers, and professors who were women hit a high point that was surpassed only in the 1970s after the implementation of policies directed at improving the occupational status of women.

Specifically political rights and obligations changed much more slowly. A number of states extended the vote to women in the last third of the nineteenth century, and in 1920 the United States became the fourteenth country to grant women the right to vote. Along with the legal right to vote, the right to choose one's representative, came greater basis for the right to hold office, to be a representative. The two major political parties were quick to seize the opportunity to try to develop their influence among the new voters. Both the Republican and Democratic parties had had women's auxiliary organizations in the presuffrage days. Both parties made attempts to equalize the representation of men and women at party conventions and party councils through the use of quota systems. Both parties endorsed the full platform of the new League of Women Voters, formerly the National American Women Suffrage Association, at their national conventions in the 1920s. Women were brought into the administrations of both Herbert Hoover and Franklin Delano Roosevelt.

Other rights and obligations took a much longer time. Women could be barred outright from jury service until 1975.[6] The criminal justice system still does not treat the two sexes in the same way either as victims or as criminals. The question of military service and obligation remains in flux. Although married women have the right to own property, the marriage and property laws of all but seven states still assume that the husband is the real property owner unless otherwise stated. In most states the domicile of a married woman is determined by the place of residence of her husband. Only fourteen states have constitutions with unequivocal statements that rights may not be denied or abridged on the basis of sex. At this writing the U.S. Constitution has no such statement, and the Supreme Court has not yet thrown its maximum possible weight behind equality for women.[7]

Although documentation of the history of formal rights and restrictions is an important basis for understanding the connections between women and politics, it is only one part of the story. Even a cursory review of what women have done and said in politics shows that the official record of women's political history, that written in laws and court decisions, tells us little about women's roles in politics.

Women and Politics Before and After the Vote

Contrary to what many people seem to think, women were not restricted exclusively to nonpolitical roles before they obtained the right to vote. The political history of women in American politics is as long as the history of the United States. Organizations such as the Daughters of Liberty, the Anti-Tea Leagues, and the Association were established by women during the American Revolution to further the patriot's cause. Women also participated on the battlefields, sometimes as fighters, but more often in the "traditional" feminine jobs of washing, cooking, mending, and nursing. Women participated in similar activities during the Civil War.

During times of peace women were particularly politically active in two types of activities: organizational volunteer work and social movements. With regard to the former, the image of the "volunteer lady" is well known. Unfortunately, however, only scant attention is paid to the instrumental role women played in establishing much of the framework for social welfare works that were later adopted by the developing welfare state. Among the groups most consistently found in the ranks of active lobbyists for reform, especially during the years of progressivism, were women's organizations.

Throughout the history of the United States women have been consistently notable in their activity and leadership in social and reform movements. Although feminism and temperance were always most closely associated with women, to underestimate the role of women in abolition, the trade union movement, and progressivism is not to understand these movements.

Women also voted when they were allowed. The earliest notable cases were in New Jersey, where a "flaw" in the statute opened the way for women to vote between 1796 and 1807, when the mistake was repaired. Beginning in 1838, when Kentucky granted white widows with children in school the right to vote in school elections, states began to extend at least limited suffrage to their female residents. A few women attempted to secure the right to vote by very direct means. These attempts were in themselves political activities. In 1648 one Margaret Brent petitioned the governor in such an effort. The petition was denied. In the 1870s more women began to take matters into their own hands. Although Susan B. Anthony's illegal attempt to vote in 1872 is well known, she was part of an organized effort in 1871 and 1872 to challenge the law under the Fourteenth and Fifteenth Amendments. One hundred fifty women across the country attempted to vote. Two cases were appealed to the Supreme Court. In *Minor* v. *Hapersett* (1875) the Court stated unequivocally that "if the courts can consider any question settled, this is one, . . . If the law is wrong, it ought to be changed; but the power for that is not with us. The arguments addressed to us bearing upon such a view of the subject may, perhaps, be sufficient to induce those having the power to make the alteration, but they ought not be permitted to influence our judgment. . . . No argument as to women's need of suffrage can be considered. We can only act upon her rights as they exist." Women had no right to vote if that right had not been extended explicitly by the state in question.

Women in the presuffrage days were by no means restricted to arenas of politics outside of parties and elections. Louis Young points out that "women were visibly part of the political environment from the innovative beginnings of modern political campaigns."[8] In many cases this meant performing tasks associated with traditional images of womanhood. When party rallies, parades, picnics, and banquets required hostesses, cooks, social organizers, and people to clean up afterward, women threw themselves into the task with all partisan fervor. Tocqueville, in his discussion of American preoccupation with politics, noted, "even the women often go to public meetings and forget household cares while they listen to political speeches."[9] He speculated that political clubs served the same purpose for American women that theaters did for women elsewhere in the world. Women also were involved in speaking, writing, and other forms of campaign activity. In his observations of American politics, Bryce seemed most impressed with women's participation. He noted the number of public letters signed by women, as well as a uniquely feminine activity: the singing of hymns outside the polls on election day to instill moralism into the day's activity.[10] These activities must be considered acts of political participation.

Women of the elite classes had greater access to power and influence than did most women. Political hostesses have long been known for their sometimes tyrannical power. Many wives of wealthy and influential men seemed to make it their business to make political suggestions and requests of their husbands upon retiring in the evening. It appears that many of these Lysistrata-like actions were successful. Sometimes attempts to influence were arranged through "conspiracies of women." Mrs. J. Borden Harriman, as she called herself, provided the following example in her recollections of her observations of the 1912 Democratic convention: "I sat not far from a pretty southern woman, who was very strong for Underwood, and was one of a group who let white doves out of baskets when he was put in nomination. By the end of the Convention she had prattled to me about her whole life-history including a love match with an elderly Congressman husband, and ended with an appeal. 'Mrs. Harriman, you seem to know all the powerful people among Wilson backers. I just wish that you'd tell them to make my husband vice-president. He is such a good man and such a clever man, and his selection would please so many people.' "[11] The memoirs of women such as Mrs. Harriman are filled with stories of attempts — often successful — to influence their families, friends, and others in political matters.

By the beginning of the twentieth century, women had entered most areas of politics. They participated in campaigns and public debates over issues, they held office in states where that was legal, they had increased their influence over a range of issues, especially those seen as congruent with the interests of women. During the quarter of a century before ratification, many manuals for female participation and citizenship were written, along with testimonies to women's political power. By 1893 Frances Willard, the President of the Women's Christian Temperance Union, was able to write, "Women have also, and notably within the last three years, secured laws for the better protection of their own sex; have immeasurably increased the property rights of married women and their rights to their children under the law; have obtained appropriations for reformatories for women and homes for those morally degraded."[12] Many began to feel they had entered the arenas of public life with nearly complete acceptance. When Mrs. Harriman was appointed in 1912 to the Federal Industrial Relations Commission, the creation of which was first urged by Jane Addams, she observed, "Most employers . . . treated me exactly as the labor representatives did, as one of the members of the Commission. The Commissioners themselves let me taste the joys of being 'just a person' instead of a lady, and took off their coats and smoked cigars, and we were all comfortable on the job together."[13] Women like Willard, Addams, and Harriman, who were ardent suffragists, seemed to feel only one obstacle stood between them and full citizenship: the vote.

The suffragists' expectations about the role the vote would play in women's lives is often misjudged. While they saw the vote as of central importance to the life of women in modern society, they were concerned with other issues as well. Most of the major long-time suffragists were involved in a variety of social movements and public oriented organizations. The most curious and instructive case is that of the extremely influential General Federation of Women's Clubs (GFWC), founded in 1890 and involving over two million members by 1910. The Federation included many of the most powerful women's organizations, and thus many of the most powerful women in politics. Many of those women felt their activities and the accolades to them by public officials were proof that women had all the power they needed. It was only in 1914 that the GFWC endorsed women's suffrage. The reason is best explained by Mary Beard in her discussion of women's involvement in municipal reform efforts:

> They have had to work to overcome the reluctance of public officials to take women seriously . . . [They] have had to enter political contests in order to place in office the kind of officials who had the wider vision; and they have had to watch without ceasing those very officials whom they have helped to elect to see that they carried out their campaign pledges. Sometimes . . . women have campaigned . . . and the ticket has been defeated. . . . Women who have experienced these political reverses have often become ardent suffragists, because . . . having been unable to influence the votes of men, they have acquired the desire and determination to cast the necessary ballots themselves.[14]

In some senses it was the women with the most political power who held off the success of the suffrage movement until after World War I. Social services, which had been in the female domain of "private philanthropy," were being adopted by the public domain, primarily at women's instigation, and women were losing power. As Beard wrote, the vote became an all important instrument for them because "Women all over the country are asking, 'Shall the control which we have hitherto been exercising be turned over to the men voters alone?' They are in increasing numbers, answering this question in the negative."[15]

Just as barring women from voting did not exclude them from politics entirely, the Nineteenth Amendment did not bring women into the political system as fully active citizens. As soon as women across the nation were allowed access to the polls, observers took note of the fact that women did not participate in elections in the same proportion as did men.

The first comprehensive empirical study of women's involvement in American politics was done by Sophinisba Breckinridge in 1933.[16]

It is, of course, very difficult to calculate sex differences in turnout without the aid of survey research, but Breckinridge does provide information on sex differences in registration in a number of cities and states. These figures show a declining difference over time, but sex difference nonetheless. In Chicago, for example, the sex differential decreased substantially from 1914, the year after Illinois granted women the right to vote in presidential elections, to 1931 (Table 2:1). Most important, however, is the evidence that the decline cannot be attributed solely to women's acceptance of their new role; during those seventeen years female registration increased by ten percentage points, but male registration decreased by ten percentage points.

Table 2:1
Percentages of Men and Women Registered to Vote in Chicago, 1914-31

	1914	1916	1920	1924	1928	1931
Men	68	64	62	62	57	58
Women	32	36	38	39	43	42
Male Advantage[a]	36	28	24	23	14	16

Source: Breckinridge, *Women in the Twentieth Century*, p. 249.

[a]"Male Advantage" is computed by subtracting the percentage of women registered from the percentage of men registered.

Although many women felt dismayed at the relatively small showing of women, others expressed more hope. Mrs. Harriman, for example, reminded her readers that "social pressures are often very, very slow. . . . The newspapers, poor dears, looked of course for something very spectacular. But then newspapers are always apt to be more interested in phenomena like meteors than in the slow growth of a mighty tree. Wait ten years, and politicians will one day wake up and say, 'Look who's here!' "[17] The development of survey research techniques after World War II provides a much better basis on which to judge "who's here" and to what degree.

If we use voting turnout as a measure, there is no indication of a steady increase in women's participation in the post–World War II era. As Table 2:2 shows there has been a considerable amount of fluctuation in both male and female turnout during that time. The net result, taking sampling error into consideration, is a relatively stable sex difference of about ten percentage points, excluding the 1968 and 1972 elections. As a point of comparison with both these figures and with Breckinridge's study, the gap between men and women in voter registration appears to have narrowed over time. In 1956 81 percent of men were registered to vote compared with 70 percent of women. In 1964 83 percent of men and 79 percent of women were registered. By 1972 80 percent of men and 77 percent were registered.[18] Other mass-level electoral activities show similarly small sex differences in the 1960s and 1970s.[19]

Table 2:2

Percentages of Men and Women Voting in National Elections, 1948-76

	1948	1952	1956	1960	1964	1968	1972	1976	1980
Men	69	72	80	80	73	69	76	78	
Women	59	62	69	69	60	66	70	69	
Male Advantage[a]	10	10	11	11	13	3	6	9	

Source: Lynn, "American Women and the Political Process," p. 406.

[a]"Male Advantage" is computed by turnout figures for females from turnout figures for males.

Survey studies also allow us to enter the world of people's perceptions of and feelings about politics. When we turn to these aspects of political involvement we find indication of a particular sense of disconnection from politics on the part of women. Women have been consistently more likely than men to agree with the statement that "politics is so complicated I can't really understand it" since 1960, when this question was first asked of the public. This difference is particularly pronounced among the college educated.[20] Similarly, women appear to feel more limited in the type of influence they can exert. Again, college-educated women are particularly more likely than college-educated men to agree with the statement that "voting is the only way I have to influence government."[21]

Although women are not substantially less involved in politics than are men, the public still does not easily associate women with the world of politics. A national survey conducted by Louis Harris and Associates in 1972 shows that the old idea that "politics is man's business" lingers.[22] These public opinion data reveal a widespread belief that women are simply not designed for full involvement in politics (Table 2:3).

Table 2:3
Attitudes toward Women's Roles in Politics, 1972

	Proportion Agreeing
Women should take care of running their homes and leave running the country up to men.	71
When it comes to politics, women don't have a mind of their own and tend to vote the way their husbands tell them to.	35
Most men are better suited emotionally for politics than are most women.	66
Politics is too dirty a business for women to become involved in.	39

Source: Louis Harris, 1972 Virginia Slims American Women's Poll.

Even if we focus exclusively on mass level politics and ignore the vast underrepresentation of women at elite levels, it appears that women are less rooted in the political system than are men despite the statement of "full opportunity" under the law. If we turn our eyes from simple descriptions of levels of participation to the problem of rootedness, or political integration, we may see the reasons.

A Newly Discovered Fragment of a Report to the Martian Anthropological Association[23]

The Hysters are a large group of people, known to have inhabited this land since the beginning of recorded time. They have always performed unique and special functions within the society, they have also been accorded a unique and special status. Numerous writers have attempted to understand the manner in which the Hysters fit into the local culture; their precise nature and role is complex and this area of anthropological inquiry has come to be called "The Mystery of Hystery" or "The Hyster Problem." Our knowledge of this group appears as follows.

The functions that the Hysters perform have been primarily service tasks. Most of these revolve around the menial labor necessary for day-to-day life maintenance, although they are employed in other service tasks as well. The latter service tasks often revolve

around the relatively unprestigious (by local standards) tasks nec-
essary for the day-to-day maintenance of business, government, and
other organizations. The most central role of the Hyster, however,
appears to be the care of children. This, above all, seems to be the
task that defines the curious status of the Hysters. We say, "curious,"
of course, because although childcare is a single task set, it seems
to be interpreted through a curious melange of values.

The Hysters appear to be at once the highest and lowest status
members of the society. Previous investigation of local rituals and
customs serve as evidence. Longstanding tradition (now falling into
disuse for reasons delineated in an earlier paper) requires that one
stand when a Hyster enters or leaves a room, that one carefully
regulate one's tone and language in the presence of a Hyster, at least
in public, and that one relieve a Hyster of the burden of perform-
ing tasks such as opening doors, and moving chairs and other light
objects. These acts do not conform to any physiological character-
istics of the Hyster, rather, they serve symbolic purposes. One is
also supposed to relieve the Hyster of the necessity of exchanging
money during social occasions, especially in public dining rooms
and places of entertainment. Indeed, it is one's duty to pay for the
privilege of participating in social occasions with a Hyster by pay-
ing for meals or entertainment. Most observers have also noted that
the Hyster loses some status as a Hyster if involved in the earning,
personal possession, or exchange of money.

Hysters are accorded great power in the community, but of very
specific types. They are central in the moral life of the community.
Although they do not hold positions of authority, they are respon-
sible in large part for the day-to-day maintenance of local moral
codes and religions. This maintenance can often be accomplished
by the smallest look or gesture of disapproval, but often stricter,
more public acts — "gossip" — are necessary. Hysters are also central
to the aesthetic life of the community. Again, their power in this
regard is restricted by and large to day-to-day roles and not to posi-
tions of authority, but the standards appear to be set and main-
tained by the Hysters. Finally, they are credited with great
peace-making powers. Once again, this power is restricted to the
day-to-day activities of individuals and small groups (there are few
if any Hysters in the government agency that determines the war
and peace policies of the society as a whole), but small arguments,

or even aggressive words can often be silenced by the mere presence of a Hyster. Often the symbols used to connote peace are images of a Hyster.

These roles, and the status accorded to them, are locally attributed to the specific physical tasks that Hysters perform, especially those related to child-rearing. A variety of myths about the origins and nature of the Hysters serve to underline the centrality of childrearing and other services in defining the other roles and the status of the Hyster.

The appearance of Hysters in positions of authority is very rare indeed. They also rarely appear in positions regarded as prestigious by the rest of the community. In this pattern lies one of the most curious aspects of the Hyster Problem: the tasks, roles, and characteristics of the Hyster are promoted as lofty but only for the Hysters. In most cases these same tasks, roles, and characteristics coincide very little with — are even antithetical to — the tasks and characteristics most valued overall. Those groups with the greatest power overall profess to "worship" Hysteric tasks and characteristics, but would feel thoroughly demeaned to be considered at all Hysteric themselves.

All of this, however, is generally known from previous research. What is of interest to us now is one of the problems that has been plaguing the community in this era of change. It appears that many of the tasks and roles, and even the characteristics of the Hysters are undergoing change. This has caused great consternation and confusion in the community because the change is very uneven and because the traditional myths of the hyster remain largely intact. The problem is nowhere more acute than in the area of politics and governance.

In recent years Hysters have been allowed to participate in the governance of the community in a formal sense for the first time. There has been an attempt to integrate them into the larger citizenry (the community is one with essentially "democratic" political institutions, found in relatively few Earth communities). It has been found, however, that despite the formal attempts to incorporate this group into the usual political processes and institutions, the Hyster's relationship to politics, the ways in which they define their relationship to politics and political issues, and especially the expectations and interpretation of their acts of citizenship remain unique to the Hysters. These seem to remain tied to the older configuration of cultural patterns of the Hyster. The political roles of the Hysters have been altered considerably, but they appear to be shaped in part by the types of patterns outlined above. There is something uneasy about the integration of Hysters into the community. In fact, some have argued that Hysters are not yet fully integrated into the political community because of the remains of the parochial culture. This has been observed a number of other times in cases where a new group has become incorporated into a political system . . . [fragment ends here].

Political Marginality and Political Integration

One of the central questions in the literature on the development of new nations or the incorporation of previously excluded groups into a political system concerns the process of political integration. As history has shown repeatedly, attainment of a markedly different political status from one previously held is not an easy process. This is especially true in the situation in which a new group, defined by shared characteristics such as race, kinship, or ethnicity, is incorporated with other groups into a political system as formally equal members. As Clifford Geertz has written, "The transfer of sovereignty from a colonial regime to an independent one is more than a mere shift of power from foreign hands to native ones; it is a transformation of the whole pattern of political life, a metamorphosis of subjects into citizens."[24] Complete integration into a new political system, or a new set of relationships to the governance of a society in which one has been a subject is a profound alteration. It necessitates cultural change.

An understanding of the process and problems of integration must be premised on an understanding of culture. As one of the people who has most influentially wrestled with the concepts of culture and integration, Geertz writes, "Believing, with Max Weber, that man is an animal suspended in webs of significance he himself has spun, I take culture to be those webs."[25] He further accepts culture as "whatever it is one has to know or believe in order to operate in a manner acceptable to its members."[26] A specific culture is defined in part by one's "primordial attachments," the assumed " 'givens' . . . of social existence [including] immediate contiguity and kin connection mainly, but beyond them the givens that stem from being born into a particular religious community, speaking a particular language, or even a dialect of a language, and following particular social practices."[27] These attachments are often of the type that appear natural, essential facts of life.

When a group's status is altered from that of outsider or subject to that of citizen, much must change if political relationships, practices, and institutions are included among or affected by those webs of significance or primordial attachments. When a group is allowed, for the first time, to participate in governing itself and others, its significance — to itself and to others — must change. It also changes in what it must know, believe, or do in order to operate in an acceptable manner.

It is a cliché to say that this process does not happen overnight or that the process of integration moves unevenly. If the metaphor of the web is an apt one, planned changes in one set of relationships, beliefs, or "significance" will reverberate to and alter others. A group that has accepted the right of political self-determination, even through institutions and processes shared by others, would probably not rest content for long with a position of being an economic underclass. On the other hand, a group that remains solidly bound in the webs of a longstanding culture may infuse its new political practices and beliefs with qualities derived from those webs. The same is true of subgroups within a country. If the process of integration is a transformation that involves the widespread sharing of certain basic attachments, beliefs, and meanings, one can see that a marked change in the political status of any group will be problematic for that group and the system as a whole.

By "any group" I am, of course, including women. Perhaps only Martian anthropologists and feminists can immediately see the similarities between women and the kinds of groups Geertz and other integration theorists discuss, but they are there. A number of people have asked whether women have a culture of their own, but rarely in the terms under consideration here.[28]

Women are born with physical characteristics that make them distinguishable as a group, and these characteristics have been interpreted by every known society to have social significance that goes well beyond the obvious physiologically based role differentiation in reproduction. Most societies interpret men and women as having different personalities, needs, temperaments, and roles in social and personal life, the economy, and politics. The precise interpretation varies from place to place and time to time, but the "significance" of sex is usually seen as natural, inevitable, and eternal.[29] These differences are supported by institutions in which people learn and enact their own social significance.

The two sexes usually have different forms of dress, different social practices, including rites of initiation, and even different languages or dialects.[30] Although women and men are obviously not segregated from each other by family or geographical locale, as is usually the case with racial, ethnic, or religious groups, there is considerably more segregation than is commonly thought to exist. As children approach the age when they become conscious of sexuality they are segregated by parents and other authority figures to increasing degrees. Just as children of different racial or ethnic groups may begin to "prefer" to play among themselves, children of different sexes do the same. Many types of leisure activities for children and adults are sex segregated. Even bars and restaurants, which can no longer legally enforce segregation, may have different "characters," some gaining reputations as "ladies luncheon places," others as "men's business places," others as places where "the boys" go. Many of the most popular social, fraternal, and service organizations are sex segregated. The job market itself remains sex segregated; men and women remain concentrated in different types of organizations. The vast amount of segregation — often self-imposed and preferred — cannot be meaningless.

Much of a person's worth is determined by how well that person conforms to the ideal for his or her gender. It is a good thing for a woman and a bad thing for a man to be very "feminine"; it is a bad thing for a woman and a good thing for a man to be very "masculine." There are profound differences between women and the usual groups for which we accept the term, "culture," but careful application of the concept in this case is far from unreasonable. If the very different significance of women and men, the amount of self-imposed segregation, the different relationships to social institutions, and the functional differentiation of the two sexes in society do not add up to some form of cultural differences, one must explain why. That women and men can love each other, be intimate with each other, and form families together does not raise enough objec-

Subtopic - Women and Voting (handwritten margin note)

tion; people of different ethnic, religious, or racial groups can and do do the same.

In 1920 the final legal door was opened to allow women to enter into the public world of politics. Women were legally transformed from subjects to citizens. They were no longer "represented" by their husbands in politics, they were now representatives of themselves. One part of the web of significance had been changed. But much of the significance of "man," "woman," and "politics" did not change, or at least changed very slowly. In this disjuncture we find the import of understanding the process of political integration.

Views of masculine society (handwritten margin note)

Politics is man's business, government is a men's club. For women, entrance into politics is not a simple matter of taking up a new activity. Rather, it is participating in activities and institutions designed and populated primarily by men, people with a different set of social norms, rituals, language, dress, and to some degree, values. Politics is imbued with values that are antithetical to those that are used to define femininity; its values are more congruent with those that are used to define masculinity.[31] Politics is a rough-and-tumble world, involving competition, aggressiveness, power, independence, rational decision-making among hard choices, and corruption. The public opinion poll cited earlier (Table 2:3) shows that even two and one-half generations after women gained their right to enter all forms of political activity, a substantial portion of the public still finds women unsuited to the world of politics. Different personality characteristics are attributed to men and women, and 66 percent of the population still felt that "most men are better suited emotionally for politics than are most women." Although women have been transformed from subject to citizen in the legal sense, they remain, in the public eye, women in the traditional significance of the concept. And politics remains political and masculine, in the traditional significance of those concepts. Women began to participate in male political activities very slowly because as Charles Merriam and Harold Gosnell found in 1924, many felt that voting simply wasn't their place.[32]

Women's "place" is not in the public world of politics, it is in the private world, especially of the family. Although it would be nearly impossible to mark the boundaries of what we call the "public" and "private," we can define the endpoints of the continuum. The public world of politics is marked by the values of rationalism, competition, judgment of value by merit, objectivity, formal social bonds, uniforms and rituals that mask the person, universalism, and a secular morality divorced from the "merciful God" and characterized at its height by *realpolitik*. In contrast, the private world of the family is marked by the values of sentiment, irrationalism, nurturance, loyalty, intimacy, love, subjectivity, sacrifice, particularism, harmony, and moralism.[33] A family unit that conforms more to the public ideal than to the private ideal — common enough today — is branded a failure. A politician who conforms to the private ideal is judged at best overly idealistic and usually a failure — or a martyr. As Jean Elshtain has demonstrated, "Individuals do not share equally in both spheres. Man, for example, has two statuses: as a public person and as a private person; therefore, men are subject to two disparate judgments in capacities as public and private persons. Woman, however, is totally immersed in the private, not public realm and is judged by the single standard appropriate to that realm alone."[34] This means that even when woman acts in the public realm of politics she is evaluated and her activities are interpreted through the values of the private realm, "she is still to be judged as a *private* person."[35] A woman's significance comes from her private roles and activities; if she loses these, she loses her "femininity," she becomes a not-woman. For this reason we speak of the "privatization" of women, referring to the imposition of private definitions or interpretations upon women even when they are engaging in public activities.[36]

Many of the objections to change in women's political roles were posed in terms of the horrors of interpreting women through public values. Women should not vote because, as Grover Cleveland said, "women will change politics less than politics will change women."[37] Ironically, as Elshtain has shown, many suffragists used the same types of arguments, suggesting that the entrance of women into politics would transform not women, but politics, that "public persons ought to be judged by the rigorous standards of the private sphere" and that their qualities would "invest the political sphere with a sanctified aura."[38] The speeches and writings of suffragists were filled with references to the "moral housekeeping" women would do in politics.[39]

Needless to say, politics has not been greatly altered by the entrance of women. We also have little reason to believe that

entrance of women into the political world has changed the definition of womanhood. Rather, it appears that women's political activities and orientations are interpreted as functions of their private
roles. Social scientists and the public alike have seen women's political roles as shaped by the values of femininity and the traditional
female roles of wifehood, motherhood, and homemaking. The spe-
cifics of these supposed relationships, as well as empirical investigation of them will be explored in later chapters, but we can suggest here that women's significance remains tied to private roles,
especially those in the family, and the political significance of
women — as interpreted by women and men — is derived from those.

The problem of political integration, then, is no more one of
simple legality of participation for women than it is for any other
new group of citizens. Women remain essentially private in the eyes
of much of the public, even when they enter the public realm. There
is, therefore, an uneasy fit between women and politics, because
"privatized" women remain anomalies in the public world of politics. Women, at least in the public eye, do not conform to a modern
political or civic role, still defined by its male leadership which,
"more than anything else seems to involve . . . a definite concept
of the public as a separate and distinct body and an attendant notion
of a genuine public interest, which though not necessarily superior
to, is dependent of and at times even in conflict with, both private
and other sorts of public interest."[40] Studies of women and politics, especially those of women as political elites, show the centrality
of conflict between the public and private in their lives, but a conflict that is due to the difficulty women face in trying to be
accepted — and accept themselves — as public persons.[41] Women, it
is said, are restricted in their public activities because their private
roles "come first." Women are also supposed to bring a unique perspective to politics (e.g., moralism, personalism) because of the
domination of their values by those derived from their private family
concerns. Political marginality is not simply a matter of women
being defined as a residual category of politics. Marginality also
exists when politics is a residual category for women. We are not
arguing here that political life should be thoroughly divorced from
private life; indeed, later we shall argue the opposite. What is at
issue is the type of connection made between public and private
life. Does the character of the connections between women's pri-

vate and public life disconnect women from politics? If women do not simply "have" private lives but, rather, are privatized, it must. Privatization breeds political marginality.

The problem of integration, therefore, is largely one of norms, values, perception, expectations; the links among these; and the relationships between these and political behavior. Taking the legal opportunity to be a citizen as a given, an analytical framework of integration focuses our attention on the role politics plays in women's lives, and especially the roles politics plays as a function or reflection of women's private roles. We have begun by focusing on women as a group because women's political status and roles are a group problem. For this part of the discussion we have looked to historical and cultural explanations. But historical and cultural explanations of the status of women as a group are not sufficient for understanding the roles of contemporary women, not just as members of a group, but as individuals, in politics. For this we will move to an empirical investigation of the relationships among women's private and public roles. Before this can be done, however, a link must be forged between cultural patterns and meanings on the one hand and women's specific role activities and orientations on the other. We therefore turn to a discussion of political socialization, the means by which individuals' behavior and orientations are developed in the context of and tied to the political and social milieu.

NOTES

1. Aileen Kraditor, ed., *Up from the Pedestal* (Chicago: Quadrangle, 1968), p. 192.
2. Mary Beard, *Women as a Force in History* (New York: Macmillan, 1946), p. 192.
3. For intellectual histories of women and politics, including these women, see Alice Rossi, ed., *The Feminist Papers: From Adams to de Beauvoir* (New York: Bantam, 1974) and Sarah Slavin Schramn, *Plow Women Rather than Reapers: An Intellectual History of Feminism in the United States* (Metuchen, N.J.: Scarecrow Press, 1979).
4. For these letters, see Rossi, *The Feminist Papers*, pp. 9-15.
5. Linda Grant de Pauw, *Founding Mothers: Women of America in the Revolutionary Era* (Boston: Houghton Mifflin, 1975), p. 200.
6. *Taylor* v. *Louisiana* 419 U.S. 522.
7. See Leslie Goldstein, *The Constitutional Rights of Women: Cases in Law and Social Change* (New York: Longman, 1979).

8. Louise Young, "Women in American Politics," *Journal of Politics* 38 (Aug., 1976), 308.
9. Alexis de Tocqueville, *Democracy in America* (New York: Doubleday, 1969), p. 243.
10. Sir James Bryce, *The American Commonwealth* (New York: Macmillan, 1914).
11. Mrs. J. Borden Harriman, *From Pinafores to Politics* (New York: Henry Holt, 1923), p. 106.
12. Frances Willard, "Women's Progress," in Lydia Hoyt Farmer, ed., *What America Owes to Women* (New York: Charles Wells Moulton, 1893), p. 286.
13. Harriman, *From Pinafores to Politics*, p. 138.
14. Mary Ritter Beard, *Women's Work in Municipalities* (New York: Appleton, 1915), pp. 46-47.
15. *Ibid.*, p. 257.
16. Sophinisba Breckinridge, *Women in the Twentieth Century: A Study of their Political, Social, and Economic Activities* (New York: McGraw Hill, 1933).
17. Harriman, *From Pinafores to Politics*, p. 351.
18. John W. Soule and Wilma E. McGrath, "A Comparative Study of Male-Female Political Attitudes at Citizen and Elite Levels," in Marianne Githens and Jewel Prestage, ed., *A Portrait of Marginality* (New York: Longman, 1977), p. 181.
19. Naomi Lynn, "Women in American Politics: An Overview," in Jo Freeman, ed., *Women: A Feminist Perspective* (Palo Alto: Mayfield, 1979), p. 411.
20. Soule and McGrath, "A Comparative Study of Male-Female Political Attitudes," p. 184.
21. *Ibid.*
22. Louis Harris and Associates, *The 1972 Virginia Slims American Women's Poll* (New York: Louis Harris and Associates, 1972). This poll is based on a national sample (N=4020).
23. From the archives of the Interterrestrial Association of Anthropologists, Feminist Division, Document #43204-E.
24. Clifford Geertz, *The Interpretation of Cultures* (New York: Basic Books, 1973), p. 269.
25. *Ibid.*, p. 5.
26. *Ibid.*, p. 11.
27. *Ibid.*, p. 259.
28. The issue of "women's culture" is an underlying theme in many recent works of feminist anthropology, literary criticism, and art history and criticism. For a journal directed to the study of women's culture, see *Chrysalis*.
29. See Shirley Ardener, ed., *Defining Females: The Nature of Women in Society* (New York: John Wiley, 1978).

30. On the differences between male and female language, see Diana Warshay, "Sex Differences in Language Style," in Constantia Salifios-Rothschild, ed., *Toward a Sociology of Women* (Lexington: Xerox, 1972), pp. 3-9; Marry Ritchie Key, *Male/Female Language* (Metuchen, N.J.: Scarecrow Press, 1975); Nancy Henley and Barrie Thorne, eds., *Language and Sex* (Rowley: Newbury House, 1975).

31. On the perpetuation of traditional definitions of masculine and feminine values and personality, see especially Inge Broverman et al., "Sex Role Stereotypes: A Current Appraisal," *Journal of Social Issues* 28 (1972), 59-78.

32. Charles Merriam and Harold Gosnell, *Nonvoting* (Chicago: University of Chicago Press, 1924).

33. The literature on the meaning of the public and private has been growing steadily. For background for this discussion, see Jean Bethke Elshtain, "Moral Woman and Immoral Man: A Consideration of the Public-Private Split and Its Political Ramifications," *Politics and Society* 4 (Winter, 1974), 453-74; Richard Sennett, *The Fall of Public Man: On the Social Psychology of Capitalism* (New York: Random House, 1976); and Robert Paul Wolff, "There's Nobody Here but Us Persons," in Carol Gould and Marx Wartofsky, eds., *Women and Philosophy* (New York: G.P. Putnam's Sons, 1976), pp. 128-44.

34. Elshtain, "Moral Woman and Immoral Man," p. 459.

35. *Ibid.*, p. 460.

36. "Privatization" is not, unfortunately, an elegant term, but there is no one word substitute.

37. Kraditor, *Up from the Pedestal*, p. xx.

38. Elshtain, "Moral Woman and Immoral Man," p. 470.

39. I have included no criticisms of the nature of the public-private split in this discussion. Such criticisms are part of the task of the concluding chapter.

40. Geertz, *The Interpretation of Cultures*, p. 309.

41. It is rarely noted that both sexes face conflicts between family and public life. The question is, how are these conflicts resolved? See Virginia Sapiro, "Public Costs of Private Commitments or Private Costs of Public Commitments? Family Roles *versus* Political Ambition," *American Journal of Political Science* 26 (May, 1982), 265-79.

CHAPTER 3

Is the Child the Mother of the Woman?
Political Socialization and Gender Roles

Most evidence provided by social scientists reinforces Simone de Beauvoir's assertion that "women are made and not born."[1] It is certainly true that about half the human species is born with at least one Y chromosome in the cells of its body and about half is not.[2] The two halves differ physically in a number of respects. Most of those born without a Y chromosome are capable of bearing children and lactating for perhaps half the length of their lives. They have one more bone, fewer red blood cells, a greater ratio of fat to muscle, proportionally smaller shoulders and wider hips, smaller overall structure, higher pitched voices, and less susceptibility to a number of diseases than do those with a Y chromosome. Most of the physical differences between the two halves are differences in proportion. Most of the functional differences exist in the reproductive organs, which are extensions of the trunk of the body in those with a Y chromosome and are protected within an escasement of muscle and bone in the trunk among those without.[3] These are some of the sex differences in human beings.

What we are concerned with here are not sex characteristics, the physical manifestations of being male or female, but gender, the socio-cultural manifestations of being a man or woman. Much of what we describe as male and female, masculine and feminine, consists of learned characteristics, expectations, and patterns of behavior. Gender is the learned significance of one's sex. Sex, or physiology, is not irrelevant to gender, but it is only part of the story. As Ann Oakley puts it, "It is true that every society uses biological sex as a criterion for the ascription of gender but, beyond that simple starting point, no two cultures would agree completely on what distinguishes one gender from the other."[4] Thus, a seventeenth-century Frenchman and a twentieth-century American man would agree they should be "manly." But they would disagree considerably over whether tights, pantaloons, beauty marks, and frills or a Brooks Brothers suit is the more natural manifestation of masculinity. "Needless to say, every society believes that its own definitions of gender corresponds to the biological duality of sex."[5]

These definitions, along with the patterns of behavior, and distributions of tasks based on these definitions, constitute gender roles. The use of the term "gender role" reinforces the point that we are talking about patterns of behavior that are learned "Despite the wealth of literature assuming that 'sex' and 'gender' are interchangeable, the primatologists persist in using the term 'sex role' correctly to describe positions in intercourse. Thus there is every reason to regard most *sociological* uses of male-female differences as involving *gender role*."[6] No single role is attached to being a man or a woman, rather, a constellation of roles, all revolving around the fact that one was born male or female. This constellation is slowly attached after the fact of physiology. Within this constellation appears to be a star that makes the significance of one's gender for one's roles in the political system. For the way in which gender roles, and especially political gender roles, are developed, we turn now to the process of socialization.

Gender Role Socialization and Politics: The Problem

The basic application of socialization theories and models to gender-related political norms and behavior is discussed at length in a number of other works.[7] The clearest conclusion that can be drawn from these studies is that the implicit and explicit messages of political gender role differentiation passed on to young people are striking. If parents enact different roles with regard to politics, children may watch and see patterns of differences between the sexes. If Daddy reads the morning newspaper while Mommy makes breakfast, or if Daddy watches the evening news while Mommy makes dinner, children may conclude that men are interested in news while women are not, even if it happens that Mommy reads the newspaper after the rest of her family leaves the house, or watches the late evening news after the dinner dishes are washed and the children are in bed. The toys and books selected for boys and girls differ considerably; those selected for boys are considerably more action and adventure oriented. The substantive content of the action and adventure is very likely to be war, spies, and international intrigue, or the general category of "cops and robbers," thus stimulating more interest in matters relating to politics in boys than in girls. School curricula and textbooks are laden with messages of political differences between the sexes. Most of the role models politics has to offer are male; women are rarely seen in any positions of power or authority in any realm. Even the female schoolteacher is likely to be supervised by a male principal. As Barbara G. Farah put it, "While Johnny is told that one day he might become President, Virginia is only reassured that there is a Santa Claus."[8]

Many studies show that children's environments are "designed" to teach them different lessons about their political roles. Fewer show convincingly that this teaching results in learning. The studies of differences in boys' and girls' political attitudes, beliefs, and activities find very few consistent differences. In the sets of studies usually cited for their investigation of sex differences, there is virtually no evidence that children's political behavior is differentiated by sex.[9] Evidence of differences in political attitudes is scant and mixed, even with regard to war and militarism, which is supposed to be one of the primary ways in which girls and boys differ.[10] Reported differences appear to be restricted primarily to political interest and knowledge. Thus, one of the most comprehensive studies of childhood gender differentiation in politics concludes, "socialization to politics does differ for boys and girls in childhood, but its effects are confined primarily to the cognitive realm."[11] This evidence is used to suggest that childhood socialization is not a strong force in shaping different political roles for males and females. In their study of high school seniors and their parents, in 1965, M. Kent Jennings and Richard G. Niemi conclude, "there are few sex differences among the parents, but those that do exist are considerably muffled in the younger generation."[12] Eight years later, however, Jennings and Niemi found that the sex differences in this generation have actually increased in many respects.[13]

The results of studies of political socialization leave open some very important questions. Why are there so few sex differences in children's political behavior and attitudes if the environment is so profoundly differentiated? Why do the differences in young childhood appear so limited in scope? How is it that sex differences actually increase in young adulthood, especially during an era of movement toward more equality between women and men? Following her review of the gender socialization literature, Lenore Weitzman suggests very briefly and tentatively that it presents an over-socialized view of women.[14] Should we revise the standard feminist view that childhood socialization has a major impact on women's political roles? In quest of this revision, this chapter focuses on the two issues in socialization research. The first concerns the translation of teaching to learning, and finally to behavior. The literature about childhood socialization appears to tell us that gender differentiated messages are *transmitted* to children, but that little evidence exists that children *learn* from these messages, and even less that children *act* upon what they have learned. The second issue is the timing of this process, the stages of role development during the course of people's lives. At what point should we see the results of gender role socialization if this process does have an effect on political roles?

Salience, Opportunity, and Childhood Socialization

The first stage in gender role development is self-classification. Girls must learn that they are girls, boys must learn that they are boys. This usually occurs by the age of three. The next step is to learn that the label, "boy" or "girl" is not the same as the label, "Dick," "Jane," or "Spot." By the age of five most children understand that the labels "boy" and "girl" are used to differentiate one category of people from another.[15] Once the confusion of gender labelling is cleared up, the process of learning the significance of those labels — the process of filling in the details of one's identity — begins in earnest. Children then learn what the differences between boys and girls are supposed to be and they learn to prefer gender "appropriate" characteristics and activities.

Children begin to exhibit gender role recognition and preference once they are capable of generalizing gender labels. By the age of five, most children are no longer under the misapprehension exhibited by Jimmy, a four year old, in the following conversation:

Johnny: I'm going to be an airplane builder when I grow up.
Jimmy: When I grow up, I'll be a Mommy.
Johnny: No, you can't be a Mommy. You have to be a Daddy.
Jimmy: No, I'm going to be a Mommy.
Johnny: No, you're not a girl, you can't be a Mommy.
Jimmy: Yes, I can.[16]

By the time children begin school they can apply male and female labels, for example, girl-women-nurse-teacher-mommy or boy-man-doctor-policeman-daddy, quite effectively. They have begun to understand gender differentiation.

Young children show an awareness of stratification as well. Stern and Searing find that children understand and recognize social class. The majority of children they questioned could tell "how important a man is" by the way he dresses, talks, or by the "kind of apartment or house he lives in."[17] Others have also found that children understand class and race stratification.[18] If children understand class and race stratification even though they are not very likely to have much social contact with children of widely divergent backgrounds, we may hypothesize that they also understand gender stratification, which is more readily apparent in their immediate world. A number of studies show that young girls and boys are well aware of gender differences in power and importance, and that they begin to take these differences as natural and proper.[19]

Of more direct relevance to evidence of the development of children's own gender roles, very young children begin to choose gender "appropriate" toys, and resist pressure to choose "incorrectly." They also begin to state a clear preference for being a member of their own sex.[20] Young school-aged children also begin to diverge in styles of interaction. It is well known that boys begin to exhibit more physical aggressiveness than do girls very early in life, but the two sexes are at least even in displays of verbal and other forms of aggressiveness. It is likely that the extra discouragement of physical outlets in girls is in part responsible for the greater verbal dexterity found in girls.[21]

The development of same-sex preference appears stronger in boys than in girls. Boys are more rigid in their preference for "boys' " toys, activities, and for male friends than girls are in their preferences for "girls' " toys, activities, and female friends. Young girls are more likely to wish they were boys than boys are to wish they were girls.[22] A number of researchers suggest that these sex differences show the effects of gender stratification, as compared with differentiation, on children. As Paul H. Mussen writes, these differences "may be a reflection of the girls' incipient awareness of the relative devaluation of the female role in the culture.[23]

Other differences between the sexes do not begin to emerge until children approach and enter adolescence. It is at this time that the physical differences between the sexes become more obvious. Moreover, adolescence marks the beginning of courtship, thus it becomes increasingly important for boys, and especially girls, to emphasize the "masculine" and "feminine" attributes that are supposed to make them attractive to the other sex. This is the time, for example, when girls and boys begin to diverge in mathematical skills, a subject which is labelled "masculine." It is important to note, however, that these differences are primarily differences in performances dependent upon the situation and setting, they are not necessarily differences in basic skills. Adolescent girls perform better on mathematical tests when the tests are administered by a woman than when they are administered by a man. Bias in textbooks and examination wording also affects apparent skill levels. When the same mathematical problem is worded with "feminine" content (e.g., sewing or baking) rather than with "male" content (surveyors measuring distances, mixing cement), clear sex differences do not emerge.[24] Of course, as further teaching takes place in a gender-biased manner, and against the resistance of girls avoiding "masculine" pursuits, eventually the skill differences will become real.

Gender differentiation takes place over a long period of time. The studies that find sex differences among young children are limited primarily to play behavior and storytelling, important childhood activities. Gender role differentiation becomes increasingly important as gender — and, eventually, sex — become more important, especially during adolescence. But thus far we have said little of politics. At what point and in what fashion does politics enter the picture?

If gender has relatively little effect on social behavior and orientations until it becomes more salient or socially relevant, how can we ask anything more of political behavior and orientations? How important is political role enactment to children? Children cannot vote and they have little direct influence over those who do. They may have different levels of political interest and may pay different amounts of attention to media coverage of politics, but their lack of understanding of the political system and certainly their lack of opportunity to participate voluntarily make direct links between gender norms learned at a young age and political behavior tenuous at best. Children do not have many opportunities to enact gender-relevant political behavior, or any type of political behavior as adults define it; their opportunity to act in or react to political affairs is severely limited by law, understanding, and the relatively close control over their activities exerted by parents and teachers. While children live under the direct authority of parents and school, the impact of the political system must remain hazy in their minds. In effect, because of the reluctance of government to "interfere" in the private domain of the home, there is only a hazy connection between what adults consider government and what is the government of the child's world. Moreover, if we are willing to believe that women hesitate before involvement in politics because "politics is man's business," we must also be willing to believe that children understand that politics is grown-ups' business.

The political system in which adults live and that within which children live can be considered closely overlapping but different arenas. If we extract and reinterpret politically relevant socialization less with the eye of the portrait painter of a bygone era who saw children merely as miniature adults and more in terms of the child's political environment, we do find evidence of gender role differentiation in political orientations and behavior. We have already noted that the bulk of childhood differentiation that has been found falls within the areas of interest and knowledge — the cognitive rather than behavioral realm. If we search for other age-appropriate acts of political behavior and perception, we find more evidence that children employ principles of gender differentiation.

Some studies show that children participate in, and many even exaggerate the gender division of political labor, especially within the family. Although the actual division of political labor between mothers and fathers is not as gender differentiated as some previously believed,[25] research by Fred Greenstein and Richard Niemi demonstrates that children's perceptions of political roles and some of their behavior are based on traditional notions of the division of labor. Greenstein reports that 48 percent of the boys and 40 percent of the girls in his sample would seek advice on voting from their fathers, while only 10 percent of the boys and 25 percent of the girls would seek advice from their mothers.[26] Greenstein suggests this pattern is due to the less political nature of women. Studies of adult political behavior do not warrant this conclusion. Sex differences in adult political behavior — even at the time Greenstein did his study — were not that great.[27] Greenstein's data might better be interpreted as demonstrations of a developing tendency for the children to use sexist principles in their political behavior, in this case, information seeking. We might also note the differences between the girls' and boys' choices. Both sexes preferred their fathers for political advice, but the margin for girls was fifteen percentage points while that for boys was thirty-eight percentage points. If the children's choices reflected the actual relative expertise of their parents, the boys' and girls' responses should not have differed so widely. Was the disparity, then, due to differences in the relative degree of identification with one or the other parent or to greater sexism on the part of boys? We cannot tell, but we have already provided evidence that boys develop more rigid gender role orientations than do girls. The likely reason is a combination of the two.

Also intriguing are the findings presented by Niemi in his study of political perception and agreement within the family. He finds that 65 percent of the high school seniors whose mothers had not voted in the previous election correctly reported this fact, while only 47 percent of the students whose fathers had not voted could do the same. Parallel analysis shows 46 percent of the children whose fathers reported the highest level of political interest identified their father's level of interest correctly, compared with 34 percent correctly reporting their mother's high level of interest.[28] The students' responses reveal the effects of prejudice in their assessment of their parents. They were more able to perceive their mothers as politically inactive and their fathers as politically interested. Their perceptions of others — even of their parents — are shaped by the traditional political gender norms they have learned. It is important to note that the data from which these findings are drawn are the same that were used for the studies of division of political labor.

Power and conflict are processes and concepts of intrinsic importance to politics. Male and female children learn to engage in both power interactions and conflict in very different ways. As discussed earlier, if one considers all forms of aggressiveness, boys and girls do not differ in their apparent need for power but boys are allowed more options for expression of aggressiveness, and thus conflict. Sex differences in styles of power and control behavior begin to emerge during childhood.[29] Children do, however, begin to associate power with men, despite the significance of female authorities such as mothers and teachers in their lives. Both sexes find it harder to believe that a woman would be a "boss" or control important resources as compared with a man.[30]

We may conclude, therefore, that childhood socialization is an important basis for the development of political gender role socialization. Children have some recognition and understanding of political gender role differentiation, but they have relatively little need or opportunity to use these principles as bases of their own political behavior and attitudes. With this observation, however, we are still confronted with a problem. If the differences between childhood and adulthood are simply matters of opportunity and salience, we remain trapped within the question of oversocialized views of women. We are left with a mechanical portrait of human development that continues to depict children as miniature adults, differentiated from adults only by size and degree. In recent years increasing numbers of scholars have pointed to the existence of socialization through the life cycle.[31] Can we continue to argue that adulthood simply reinforces and forces into the open norms and patterns of behavior learned in childhood?

The process of change over the life cycle can appear as mere mechanical reinforcement only if one narrowly views childhood socialization with the exclusive intent of finding the roots of gender differentiation. The typical mode of feminist analysis of socialization is to do precisely this, combing through agents of childhood socialization to find evidence of transmission of sexism. As discussed earlier, it is not difficult to find that most agents of childhood socialization are transmitting strong messages of gender differentiation. Indeed, they are. If we open our view to the full range of

messages transmitted to little girls, however, we find that the reper-
toire of messages they receive is by no means limited to the stereo-
typically feminine. Although the "hidden curriculum" is strongly
biased toward gender differentiation, girls are exposed to the same
parents, teachers, and schoolbooks as are boys, and roughly the
same mass media. They, too, hear about American folk heroes and
they, too, hear about the values of independence, achievement, and
the other norms generally thought of as masculine. They are certainly subjected to training in the dominant values of American
political culture. Although, as we have seen, the shaping of gender
differentiation begins at a very young age, we might argue that girls
are subject to less constraint than are women. Here, however, we
refer not only to physical and behavioral constraint, but to psychological constraint as well.

When students of socialization discuss learning and cognitive development, they generally focus on learning and development of
new skills and values. "Socialization" should refer not only to the
learning of basic values and behavior, but also to the development
of structures of values and behavior, that is, belief systems or
ideology and roles. Thus, we can argue that in childhood a large
range of values is learned, but a considerable portion of what we
might identify as adult socialization is the learning of what weight
should be assigned to different values and goals, which norms should
be applied through behavior in specific situations, and, given particular hierarchies of norms or values, what type of behavior is called
for in a given situation. We have already seen that little girls exhibit
considerable flexibility in their gender roles and preferences, especially when compared with boys. We have also seen that they appear
to comprehend that a higher value is attached to things "masculine." What remains for adulthood, in large part, is the development of structure.

Responsibility and Adult Socialization

Over a century ago Alexis de Tocqueville made note of the con-
tinuities and discontinuities in learning and enactment of social
norms during the course of women's life cycles. In his discussion
of the roles and duties of women in America, he argued that young
girls know to some degree what will be expected of them as wives

and mothers—that is, they have been socialized to the nature of women's roles—but as children and youths they are allowed immense freedom. "While there is less constraint on girls than anywhere else, a wife submits to stricter obligations." He argues that "public opinion carefully keeps women within the little sphere of domestic interests and duties and will not let her go beyond them."[32]

> When she is born into the world the young American girl finds ideas firmly established; she sees the rules that spring therefrom; she is soon convinced that she cannot for a moment depart from the usages accepted by her contemporaries without immediately putting in danger her peace of mind, her reputation and her very social existence, and she finds the strength required for such an act of submission in the firmness of her understanding and the manly habits inculcated by her education.[33]

Tocqueville's observations raise three important points. First, gender-based norms are "firmly established" rules and principles that a young girl must learn. Second, although Tocqueville knows that the child learns the rules, she does not have to call them into action as often as she will in the future. The third point that Tocqueville suggests is that adulthood is also a time for basic learning of the type we may label socialization. That is the time when one learns more clearly about the consequences of one's actions, when one comes to understand much more the value of responsibility, and the activities of how norms are to be enacted.

Roles contain rules for social behavior and interaction. Children and adolescents test the rules—often by stretching and breaking them. In adulthood the rules are taken more seriously. Enforced by public opinion, as Tocqueville called it, reinforced by a sense of responsibility, these rules or roles become more important. "What in adolescence may be a forgivable relapse, indicating that one is not quite ready but must try again, becomes in adulthood a serious failure which is not easily forgiven and may not admit of repeated trials. The adolescent must 'put off childish things,' renounce adolescent indulgences, and accept serious adult responsibilities."[34] The advent of responsibility as a motivation for role conformity is not simply a function of adulthood; rather, it is an effect of specific role enactment. Hill and Aldous, in a discussion of the effects of marriage and parenthood on role enactment, write, "With the advent of parenthood, the trial period [of the marriage] is over. The couple is now responsible for a younger generation which represents the continuity of the unit."[35] Changes in responsibility are direct functions of life cycle events such as marriage, parenthood, or shifting the burden of support from parents to self.[36] Adults become more independently responsible for their lives and the lives of significant others through assumption of gender-typed adult roles. Although parents and teachers try to teach responsibility to children, in the end the adult world is considerably more designed to instruct people about the consequences of nonconformity to important principles. The norms of reward and punishment, rights and obligations are not the same in the child's family as they are in the adult's occupational and political world.[37] Conformity to general cultural norms, specifically enacted through social, political, and economic institutions, is a life-and-death matter in adulthood. In most aspects of day-to-day existence, however, it is not the immediate threat of punishment that maintains adult conformity. Rather, the adult norms become internalized in a desire to be a "good parent," "good wife," "good worker," or "good citizen." Adult responsibility means knowing what is expected of one and fulfilling that expectation. The two most important institutions in which adults act out their lives — the family and the work setting — are entered into by contract, which obliges the individual to fulfill his or her duties. The very word, "responsibility" (and not coincidentally, the word, "spouse") is derived from a root word meaning, "to pledge" or "to promise."

The concept of adult responsibility does not imply that adult role structures are simply mechanical enforcers of norms learned in childhood. First, enactment and balancing of adult roles means that the norms embedded in them are given structure and are reinterpreted by the individual in order to put them into use. Second, although adult roles serve as enforcers of childhood norms, any simple relationship between childhood learning and adult behavior may be obscured by the socialization effects of adult roles as well as by historical changes taking place in society.

One of the reasons it appears to be so difficult to assess the political socialization effects of adult participation in private institutions such as the family is the completeness with which many people assume children are socialized into acceptance and fulfillment of anticipated adult private roles. Adult political roles may be taught to children in the abstract, indirectly, or by analogy. Adult family roles and personal values, it is assumed, can be taught much more directly and forcefully. This assumption is applied particularly to the case of women's family roles. Talcott Parsons, the eminent student of family roles and interaction, provides a good example of this reasoning: "It is possible from an early age to initiate girls directly into many important aspects of the adult female role. Their mothers are continually about the house and the meaning of many of the things they are doing is relatively tangible and easily understandable to a child. It is also possible for the daughters to participate actively and usefully in many of these activities." In comparison, "many of the masculine functions are of relatively abstract and intangible character, such that their meaning must remain almost wholly inaccessible to the child."[38] If girls are the subjects of such complete socialization to predominant private roles, there would be little point in discussing the distinct political impact of those adult roles. If, on the other hand, there is more disjuncture than Parsons, among others, suggests, the study of political socialization must turn more directly to the links between adult family roles and political roles.

Anticipatory socialization is an important concept, but one which must be used with caution. As Roberta Sigel and Marilyn Hoskin write, "It is one thing to watch a father leave in the morning, briefcase or lunchpail in hand, and imagine the role of a breadwinner; it is quite another to be one."[39] Despite Parsons's suggestion to the contrary, it is also one thing to watch a mother perform her daily tasks and imagine being a mother; it is quite another to be one. If we look back to Parsons's observations of family roles, and especially women's roles, we can see more clearly the disjunctures, and especially those relevant to political socialization.

The first point is that by "adult female role" Parsons meant, of course, the homemaker. When Parsons wrote his analysis of the family, about two-thirds of American women were homemakers. Now about half are homemakers, and the figure drops even lower among women whose children are at least of school age. Even when Parsons wrote, a large proportion of women were not "continually about the house" and available to be observed; now, especially counting part-time employment, even fewer are. If we add to this situation the observation that from an early age children are in school for a considerable portion of the day and that women's work often continues after children are in bed or begins before they wake up, we reduce greatly the amount of time children can spend observing the tasks of the homemaker and even, we might add, the mother.

Assuming, for the moment, that children can observe a significant portion of homemaking tasks, there are still reasons for doubting the existence of as easy and complete a transmission of role from mother to daughter as Parsons suggests. One revolves around the question of the degree to which women's domestic roles remain the same from one generation to the next. Many people seem to assume that domestic roles of women have remained essentially the same over time, that only the time they take has been reduced by technological developments.[40] In fact, the reverse is true. Studies of time use show that the time spent on housework increased between the beginning of the century and the present and that the presence of labor-saving devices appears to be associated with an increase in the amount of time spent on housework; only one study shows a decrease in time spent on housework, and that is John Robinson's study of the time between 1965 and 1975, when the average time dropped by twenty-two minutes a day.[41] It should be noted that the amount of time men spent on housework also declined during that period. The time spent in household labor is little understood. Sociologists like Parsons sometimes observe that the demands of men's work leaves little time for other pursuits while the housewife role "scarcely approaches a full time occupation for a vigorous person."[42] In contrast, Joann Vanek finds that by taking all forms of work into consideration, the work week is 56 hours long for married women who are not employed, 62.5 hours for men who are employed, and 71 hours for married women who are employed. Considering only families with young children, employed women have 80-hour work weeks compared with 65 hours for married men.[43]

Although the time women spend on housework has not undergone dramatic changes from one generation to the next, we can argue that the role itself changes quite considerably and that it cannot be transmitted very simply.[44] First, technological changes have not reduced time to any great extent, but they have changed the composition of tasks. Second, we may consider the geographic mobility of Americans from generation to generation during the last century. Taking into account immigration, shifts from the ports of entry to second-generation communities, shifts from rural to urban areas and from urban to suburban areas alone, the manner in which domestic tasks are carried out must have been greatly altered. Third, demographic changes from mother to daughter in education, occupational commitments, and numbers and timing of children have affected domestic roles. Fourth, economic conditions both of the family and of the society alter the work a homemaker must do. The fewer the financial resources of a family, the more women's labor in the home must increase to compensate for decreased availability of consumer goods, including food, clothing, and entertainment for children. Finally, and in large part as a result of societal-level changes, the norms delineating what a homemaker should do vary from time to time. The advent of home economics courses in schools provided new norms for nutrition. Changes in the forms and quantity of energy available for family consumption are not simply the result of technological developments; they are also moderated by advertising campaigns. One generation is told to use, another to save. The same is true of food and other goods. Norms defining "good" childcare have changed as well.

As the foregoing points should suggest, the homemaker role, like other roles, is not simply a list of tasks that must be accomplished; it also has an underlying component of norms and values that define both the role and the person occupying it. Thus, whereas children may, as Parsons assumed, observe some of the tasks of the homemaker, much of the role is of the same abstract and intangible character as other jobs. Indeed, it is plausible to argue that while jobs performed outside the home (and therefore invisible to the child) may only be understood in abstract and symbolic terms, familiarity and constant presence of the homemaker in the child's world may force the tasks, and especially the child-oriented tasks, to overshadow the full meaning and definition of the homemaker role. To use an old cliché, the forest is missing for the trees. The fact that men seem to have so little comprehension of what their homemaker wives do even though they were once children in a homemaker's home bears witness to what some have called the "invisibility" of the role.

The homemaker role may be one that is most strongly encouraged for women in comparison with other work roles, but psychological studies show it is not necessarily a "natural fit" for women. Psychological evidence reveals the difficulty women have in adjusting to being housewives as well as the negative effects of the role on women. Housewives exhibit more symptoms of psychological distress as well as lower senses of self-esteem than do other married women.[45] Homemakers have higher rates of "middle-aged depression" after their children leave home than do employed women.[46] If women were well prepared for homemaking, would it be such a shock to the system?

Although we have discussed only homemaking, we might make the same analysis of marital and maternal roles as well. Research on the family shows that in both of these cases women have more to learn from entering and fulfilling these roles than they learned as children.[47] Certainly one of the things that must be learned is how to manage conflict among the different domestic roles. Where sociologists and psychologists have discussed female role conflict, they have generally restricted themselves to analysis of conflict between public roles and private roles. What is rarely pointed out is that the demands and responsibilities of motherhood, for example, are not always compatible with the demands and responsibilities of wifehood. Even within the domestic arena the structures and interrelationships of different roles and values must be learned during adulthood.

If domestic roles are sources of value learning and structuring during adulthood, other occupational roles must be as well. But whereas we can argue that domestic roles may be greater agents of socialization than is commonly assumed, employment may in fact be less influential than is often thought.[48] Discussion of socialization through employment must take account of segregation in the labor market. Women and men remain segregated to a large extent in very different jobs, and characteristics of female and male employment are consistent with the values of masculinity and femininity. The majority of employed women are found in jobs (whether blue collar, white collar, or professional) occupied primarily by women. Three-quarters of employed women are concentrated in fifty-seven jobs, and thirty-one of those jobs are 75 percent female.[49] Women's occupations tend to emphasize values traditionally associated with femininity, including nurturance, service, docility, and subordination. Thus, although we should expect employment to help shape women's values and roles, the direction of the effects

Something not of politics

may not be uniformly away from the norms of traditional gender role differentiation and stratification.

Socialization and Integration

Essentially undifferentiated male and female infants are quickly shaped to become more differentiated boys and girls and, eventually, even more differentiated men and women. Basic norms of masculinity and femininity are learned by young children and, as these norms become more critical to the way one is expected to behave in social settings, they become enforced with increasing vigor by the institutionalization of adult gender roles. These roles not only refer to activities pursued by men and women, they also define men and women. Thus a woman does not simply give birth to a child, she becomes a mother. She does not simply carry on activities that are necessary for day-to-day maintenance of human life, she becomes a housewife. She does not simply participate in a ceremony that marks acceptance of a particular kind of relationship with a man, she becomes a wife. Each of these roles institutionalizes particular aspects of gender-relevant norms. Wifehood enforces dependency and self-sacrifice, especially with regard to men, motherhood enforces nurturance, self-sacrifice, and the centrality of children in women's lives, and homemaking provides the form and substance of female labor and women's relationship to the economy.

Subsequent and more peripheral roles — including those in politics — must be shaped to some degree by the imperatives of gender roles. In a sense we are arguing that while children are not merely passive objects of socialization agents, adults are even more active in their own socialization, in the way they integrate their different activities and responsibilities, and in the way, therefore, they both integrate themselves into and help create more general cultural patterns. The cultural, historical, and macro-level concerns raised in Chapter 1 and the more individual level, social-psychological concerns raised in this chapter are not independent. Both must be taken into account in trying to understand how women, either as a group or as individuals, are integrated into the political world.

We have narrowed our view to the world of adults. This is not to argue that childhood socialization is unimportant; as argued here repeatedly the child is, to a large degree, the mother of the woman.

We have argued, however, that the effects of adult gender roles on the development of patterns of political behavior and attitudes have been underplayed and to some degree misconstrued. Further, we have done little more than to hint at what some of the substantive connections between private gender roles and political roles might be. It is to those relationships that we turn for the remainder of the book.

NOTES

1. Simone de Beauvoir, *The Second Sex* (New York: Alfred Knopf, 1952).
2. The following is, of course, the barest outline of the physical differences between sexes. For more information, written in a manner that is accessible to nonbiologists, see John Money and Anke A. Ehrhardt, *Man and Woman, Boy and Girl* (Baltimore, Md.: Johns Hopkins University Press, 1972) and Ruth Hubbard, Mary Sue Henifin, and Barbara Fried, eds., *Women Look at Biology Looking at Women* (Cambridge: Schenkman, 1979). The latter especially emphasizes the effects of interaction of the social world and human physiology.
3. I describe the placement of the reproductive organs in this manner because male organs are usually described incorrectly, as "external," while female reproductive organs are described as "internal." Much symbolic mileage has been derived from the "internal-external" dichotomy. "Internal" should refer to parts of the body encased within the external epidermis, as the male reproductive organs are. The muscles of the penis are no more "external" than are the muscles of the leg or the arm. To view the male organs as external to the body is an indication of a curious interpretation, perhaps alienation, of the reproductive organs in men.
4. Ann Oakley, *Sex, Gender, and Society* (New York: Harper and Row, 1972), p. 158.
5. *Ibid.*, p. 158. "The duality of sex" is itself not completely correct; we use dichotomy male-female for what is really a continuum. See Money and Ehrhardt, *Man and Woman, Boy and Girl.*
6. David Tresemer, "Assumptions Made about Gender Roles," in Marcia Millman and Rosabeth Moss Kanter, eds., *Another Voice: Feminist Perspectives on Social Life and Social Choice* (Garden City: Doubleday, 1975), p. 309. See also Oakley, *Sex, Gender, and Society.* For more discussion, see Chapter 4, this volume.
7. For general discussion of gender role socialization, see especially Eleanor Maccoby, ed., *The Development of Sex Differences* (Stanford: Stanford University Press, 1966); Lenore J. Weitzman, *Sex Role Socialization* (Palo Alto: Mayfield Publishing, 1979), and Irene Frieze et al., *Women and Sex Roles: A Social Psychological Perspective* (New

York: W.W. Norton, 1978). On gender and political socialization, see Veronica Stolte Heiskanen, "Sex Roles, Social Class, and Political Consciousness," *Acta Sociologica* 14 (1971), 83-95; Robert Dowse and John Hughes, "Girls, Boys, and Politics," *British Journal of Sociology* 22 (Mar., 1971), 53-67; Jennifer S. MacLeod and Sandra T. Silverman, *"You Won't Do:" What Textbooks on U.S. Government Teach High School Girls* (Pittsburgh: Know, 1973); Lynn Iglitzin, "The Making of Apolitical Woman," in Jane Jaquette, ed., *Women and Politics* (New York: Wiley, 1974), pp. 25-36; M. Kent Jennings and Richard G. Niemi, *The Political Character of Adolescence* (Princeton: Princeton University Press, 1974); Jan Morgan, "Woman and Political Socialization; Fact and Fantasy in Easton and Dennis and in Lane," *Politics* 9 (May, 1974), 50-55; Anthony Orum, Roberta Cohen, Sherri Grasmuck, and Amy Orum, "Sex, Socialization, and Politics," *American Sociological Review* 39 (Apr., 1974), 197-209.

8. Barbara G. Farah, "Climbing the Political Ladder: The Aspirations and Expectations of Female Partisan Elites," in Dorothy McGuigan, ed., *New Research on Women and Sex Roles* (Ann Arbor: CEW, 1976), p. 238.

9. See especially Iglitzin, "The Making of Apolitical Woman"; Jennings and Niemi, *The Political Character of Adolescence*; Orum et al., "Sex, Socialization, and Politics."

10. Howard Tolley, *Children and War: Political Socialization to International Conflict* (New York: Teachers College Press, 1973).

11. Orum et al., "Sex, Socialization, and Politics," p. 207.

12. Jennings and Niemi, *The Political Character of Adolescence*, p. 306.

13. M. Kent Jennings and Richard G. Niemi, *Generations and Politics: Young Adults and Their Parents* (Princeton: Princeton University Press, 1981).

14. Weitzman, *Sex Role Socialization*, pp. 80-85.

15. For reviews of early childhood learning, see Maccoby, *The Development of Sex Differences*; Weitzman, *Sex Role Socialization*; Frieze, *Women and Sex Roles*.

16. Reported by Lawrence Kohlberg, "A Cognitive-Developmental Analysis of Children's Sex-Role Concepts and Attitudes," in Maccoby, *The Development of Sex Differences*, p. 95.

17. Donald Searing and Alan Stern, "The Stratification Beliefs of British and American Adolescents," *British Journal of Political Science* 6 (Apr., 1976), 177-203.

18. Roberta G. Simmons and Morris Rosenberg, "Functions of Children's Perception of the Stratification System," *American Sociological Review* 36 (Apr., 1971), 235-49; Jeannette Tudor, "The Development of Class Awareness in Children," *Social Forces* 49 (June, 1971), 470-76; Chris L. Kleinke and Tara A. Nicholson, "Black and White Children's Awareness of de Facto Race and Sex Differences," *Developmental Psychology* 15 (Jan., 1979), 84-86.

19. For example, Kleinke and Nicholson, "Black and White Children's Awareness."
20. Weitzman, *Sex Role Socialization,* Chapters I and II.
21. Eleanor Maccoby and Carol Jacklin, *The Psychology of Sex Differences* (Stanford: Stanford University Press, 1974).
22. Kohlberg, "A Cognitive Developmental Analysis."
23. Paul H. Mussen, "Early Sex Role Development," in David Goslin, ed., *Handbook of Socialization Theory and Research* (New York: Rand McNally, 1969), p. 711.
24. Diana Ruble et al., "Sex Differences in Personality and Abilities," in Frieze, *Women and Sex Roles,* pp. 61-62.
25. M. Kent Jennings and Kenneth P. Langton, "Mothers vs. Fathers: The Formation of Political Orientations among Young Americans," *Journal of Politics* 31 (May, 1969), 329-58; Jennings and Richard G. Niemi, "The Division of Political Labor between Mothers and Fathers," *American Political Science Review* 65 (Mar., 1971), 69-82; Paul Allen Beck and Jennings, "Parents as 'Middlepersons,' " *Journal of Politics* 37 (Feb., 1975), 83-107.
26. Fred I. Greenstein, *Children and Politics* (New Haven: Yale University Press, 1969), p. 119.
27. John W. Soule and Wilma E. McGrath, "A Comparative Study of Male-Female Political Attitudes at Citizen and Elite Levels," in Marianne Githens and Jewel Prestage, eds., *A Portrait of Marginality: The Political Behavior of the American Woman* (New York: Longman, 1977), pp. 178-95.
28. Richard G. Niemi, *How Family Members Perceive Each Other* (New Haven: Yale University Press, 1974), pp. 66-68.
29. Dorothea D. Braginsky, "Machiavellianism and Manipulative Interpersonal Behavior in Children," *Journal of Experimental Psychology* 6 (1970), 77-99.
30. Kleinke and Nicholson, "Black and White Children's Awareness."
31. Jennings and Niemi, *The Political Character of Adolescence;* Jennings and Niemi, *Generations and Politics;* Neil Cutler, "Demographic, Social-Psychological, and Political Factors in the Politics of Aging: A Foundation for Research in 'Political Gerontology,' " *American Political Science Review* 71 (Sept., 1977), 1011-25.
32. Alexis de Tocqueville, *Democracy in America* (Garden City: Doubleday, 1969), p. 592.
33. *Ibid.,* p. 593.
34. Talcott Parsons, *Essays in Sociological Theory* (New York: Macmillan, 1954), p. 90. For further discussion of Parsons on responsibility, see Walter B. Roettger, "Parsons, Behavioralism, and the Notion of Responsibility," *Emporia State Research Studies* 25 (Spring, 1977), 5-33.
35. Reuben Hill and Joan Aldous, "Socialization for Marriage and Parenthood," in Goslin, *Handbook of Socialization Theory and Research,* p. 923.

36. Ester Sales, "Women's Adult Development," in Frieze, *Women and Sex Roles*, especially pp. 169-70.
37. Richard Merelman, "The Family and Political Socialization: Toward a Theory of Exchange," *Journal of Politics* 42 (May, 1980), 461-86.
38. Parsons, *Essays in Sociological Theory*, p. 92.
39. Roberta Sigel and Marilyn Hoskin, "Perspectives on Adult Socialization — Areas of Research," in Stanley Renshon, ed., *Handbook of Political Socialization: Theory and Research* (New York: Macmillan, 1977), p. 263.
40. Parsons, *Essays in Sociological Theory*, p. 98.
41. John P. Robinson, "Household Technology and Household Work," in S. F. Berk, ed., *Women and Household Labor* (Beverly Hills: Sage, 1980), pp. 53-68. This essay also contains an excellent review of the relevant time use studies.
42. Parsons, *Essays in Sociological Theory*, p. 98.
43. Joann Vanek, "Household Work, Wage Work, and Sexual Equality," in Berk, *Women and Household Labor*, p. 277.
44. For works on household labor, see Ann Oakley, *The Sociology of Housework* (New York: Random House, 1974); Berk, *Women and Household Labor*; Helena Z. Lopata, *Occupation: Housewife* (New York: Oxford, 1971).
45. For a review, see Carol Tavris and Carole Offir, *The Longest War: Sex Differences in Perspective* (New York: Harcourt, Brace, Jovanovich, 1977), pp. 222-25.
46. For a review, see Juanita Williams, *Psychology of Women: Behavior in a Biosocial Context* (New York: W.W. Norton, 1977), pp. 360-68.
47. See especially Jessie Bernard, *The Future of Marriage* (New York: Bantam, 1972); Bernard, *The Future of Motherhood* (New York: Penguin, 1974); Bernard, *Women, Wives, Mothers* (Chicago: Aldine, 1975); Lopata, *Occupation: Housewife*.
48. For research on women and employment, see Alice H. Amsden, ed., *The Economics of Women and Work* (New York: Penguin, 1980) and Karen Wolk Feinstein, ed., *Working Women and Families* (Beverly Hills: Sage, 1979).
49. Sharlene J. Hesse, "Women Working: Historical Trends," in Feinstein, *Working Women and Families*, pp. 35-62.

CHAPTER 4

Beyond Sex Differences: Empirical Analysis of Gender Roles

The amount of research on women's roles in and relationships to the political system has increased dramatically in recent years. For many reasons this growth is a good thing; it reflects a renewed concern for understanding the gender relevant aspects of women's and men's political lives and has resulted in an awareness of these aspects that we once lacked. This rapid growth has its drawbacks, however. Our knowledge of women's roles in politics has increased but there has been little time to re-examine or re-evaluate much of the new work. As a result, there is little in the way of critical discussion of appropriate methods for undertaking empirical research on women's relationships to politics.

The mode of analysis selected for the remainder of this study is survey research. Before turning to an explanation of the specific approach taken here, this chapter offers a review and discussion of current procedures in survey research on women and politics.

Sex Differences

One of the most common approaches to the study of women and politics employs comparison of men as a group with women as a group. These studies compare, for example, the percentage of men who vote with the percentage of women who vote, the percentage of girls who are interested in politics with the percentage of boys who are interested in politics. This seems, after all, a logical approach. Our best comparative impulses tell us that in order to study women properly we must compare them with someone else; men seem the likely candidates.

The reasons for using comparisons based on the variable "sex" seem crystal clear — at first. Further thought obscures the clarity. What does this variable mean? What do we learn when we compare males as a group with females as a group?

We have to specify in more than intuitive terms the reasons for using "sex" as the major independent variable in women's studies. If we treat women and men as two distinct groups, we assume at minimum that we are interested in comparing one collection of people who share specific characteristics. What are those distinct characteristics of women and men which are assumed to be politically relevant? Let us review the possibilities.

The most obvious characteristic that distinguishes and differentiates men and women is physiology. But most students of women and politics do not claim to be bio-political scientists; that is, they provide no indication that they are using "sex" as an indicator of physiological characteristics in their studies of political attitudes and behavior. Indeed, most political scientists would be most unqualified to carry out the type of research appropriate to such questions.

The variable "sex" may be used to indicate important psychological characteristics: "masculinity" and "femininity." But sex is a dichotomous variable, whereas masculinity-femininity is not. Masculinity and femininity are ideal types, fixed and opposite ideals, with "reality" distributed in the range in between.[1] Rather than thinking of masculinity and femininity as cultural ideals to which people adhere to only limited degrees, the variable "sex" can structure the researcher into maintaining male and female as fixed, mutually exclusive opposites. For this reason those who don't fit are often labelled "deviants" or "cross-sex" actors, thus framing these concepts as something other than the cultural constructs they are. Psychological research shows that there is considerably more variation in personality characteristics within the sexes than there is across the sexes. Thus, using the variable "sex" as an indicator of personality traits is empirically incorrect.

Another way to understand "sex" is that it summarizes two different kinds of experiences or roles. There are roles played predominantly by women (wife, housewife, mother, prostitute, teacher of little children) and roles played predominantly by men (husband, truck driver, doctor, teachers of big children). As discussed earlier, women and men remain relatively segregated in different sectors of the economy. In the end, "male-female" is usually translated as "male (husband, father, employed person)-female (wife, mother, homemaker)." This conceptualization conceals both lack of clarity and erroneous assumptions. Not all women are wives, mothers, or housewives. Indeed, only a small minority of the adult American female population fit the description, "wife, mother with children at home, housewife." A summary category that summarizes considerably less than half the people who fall in that category is not very useful.

Another problem with the study of "sex differences" is that this type of research can make it more difficult for the researcher to transcend the tradition of male-oriented investigation. Many scholars have discussed what has been labelled a "masculist" or "male" bias in research, the acceptance of what is male as the norm.[2] The tendency to view men as the standard by which women are evaluated takes a number of forms. The bulk of research on women performed by nonfeminist scholars may be classified as part of the Henry Higgins school of analysis. In the Higgins school one asks, "Why can't a woman be more like a man?" or "Why are women so much like men?" In "sex differences" research the Henry Higgins ideology emerges in the primary questions that are asked and the major conclusions that are drawn. A few examples follow.

In the case of political participation, male levels of political participation are accepted as full participation. Thus if 40 percent of men vote in a particular election, and 40 percent of women do the same, reports will usually conclude that women are fully integrated into the political system. This conclusion is even more curious than that of economists who tell us that if 6 percent of adult Americans are without jobs we have "full employment." In our example, political integration becomes a shifting measure depending on what men are doing, just as full employment is a shifting measure depending on the ideology of the economist in charge. A slightly different interpretation is offered when the subject is husbands and wives rather than men and women. When told that husbands and wives vote the same way, many people jump to the conclusion that this is a display of male opinion leadership or female submissiveness, even though sex differences of this sort tell us nothing about causality.

Even more curious are the Higgins conclusions drawn when women are more active than are men in a particular activity or when they think differently than do men. Thus, for example, Robert Lane refers to women's participation in reform activities as motivated by a "bloodless love of the good"; their activities are, to him, apolitical and peculiar.[3] Robert Dahl contrasts male and female motivations for involvement in school politics through the PTA by labelling the women's activity more social or personal.[4] Fred Greenstein labels little boys' interest in war "political" and calls little girls' interest in "getting rid of bad people" nonpolitical.[5]

Although we have argued that men's and women's lives differ to a considerable degree, and that men and women are treated differently, more specific understanding of the relationship of gender roles to politics requires that we move beyond assuming that research on sex differences is always the appropriate way to study women and politics. It is not *necessarily* appropriate if our concern is to understand the dynamics of gender *roles*. Sex differences research is helpful only when we want to know about sex differences. That is not the question here.

Because simple demonstrations of the presence or absence of sex differences in political behavior or attitudes do not answer the question of the effects of role variations, many people have turned to direct investigation of the effects of marital, parental, or employment status on political roles. Some problems of clarity and precision remain with the common modes of this type of analysis as well. These are outlined below.

First, we tend to measure gender roles through the use of check-off categories of status. Knowing that a person is married, childless, or a housewife tells us only part of the story of his or her role composition. Within the categories of single, married, divorced, or cohabiting, for example, a wide variety of marital roles might exist. These may vary systematically from one subcommunity to another, or from one life-cycle phase to another. Status categories do not go very far in describing real variations in roles.

A second problem has to do with the meaning of the concept "role effects." If there is reason to suspect a relationship exists between gender roles and political roles, we must also consider at least one of two possibilities. The first is that specific gender roles provide or extract resources that are necessary for specific political roles.

These might include time, energy, access to communication net-works, money, or status. The second is that norms, values, needs, or expectations inherent in specific gender roles are congruent with or similar to norms, values, needs or expectations inherent in specific political roles.

A role is a set of patterned activities, but it is also, as discussed earlier, the institutionalization of a set of norms. Thus we could pose a number of specific hypotheses regarding the relationship of one specific familial role to politics. Motherhood serves as a good example. It has been argued that motherhood depresses the level of women's political activities in some respects because of the time and energy demands required of mothers.[6] It has also been argued that motherhood promotes interest in specific types of political issues, or fosters particular political values because of women's attention to the substantive concerns revolving around children.[7] Both of these aspects of gender roles must be considered distinctly.

A final problem with many studies of gender roles and politics is that investigations of these relationships often tend to focus on single roles considered in isolation, for example, motherhood *or* marriage. This type of selective investigation goes only part way toward untangling the vast web of interrelated roles. People who are married also tend to have children, at least half the women who are married are also employed, and so on. If we simply compare mothers and childless women without taking other roles into account, how do we know we are observing the effects of mother-hood *per se* as opposed to marital status, which is highly corre-lated with maternal status? We do not want to lump all women together regardless of their roles; neither do we want to examine specific roles in isolation from consideration of other related roles.

These admittedly general observations of problems of approaches to survey research on women and politics serve as the underpinnings of the treatment used for the remainder of this book. The rest of this chapter outlines the specific methodology employed here and begins to offer an empirical consideration of women's roles and politics.

Design and Methodology

The empirical problem we have set for ourselves is the follow-ing: In what ways do women's private roles shape the form and substance of their involvement in politics at the citizen level? Each of the succeeding chapters focuses on a specific aspect of political involvement. Specific hypotheses are drawn in rather unorthodox fashion. Because of the unusually high suffusion of social science treatments of women and politics with cultural stereotypes and popular conventional wisdom, and the relative lack of consensus about scientifically based "standing truths" in the field of women's studies, the hypotheses emerge from a variety of types of sources, often including those rarely used explicitly in the normal sciences of society. If as feminist scholars claim, much of what we call "conventional wisdom" is mere stereotype, this wisdom can only be dismissed convincingly if we reincarnate the statements of such "wisdom" into hypotheses that are subject to falsification. From the point of view of those who are skeptical about the statements of feminist scholars, the same treatment applies.

The research is based on data drawn from the University of Michigan Panel Socialization Study. In 1965 the Survey Research Center (SRC) launched a socialization study for which a national probability sample of 1,669 high school seniors, representative of high school seniors in the nation as a whole, were interviewed. In 1973 the original sample served as the basis of a second wave of interviews, which included many of the same questions that were asked in the original study. At that time 1,119 reinterviews were obtained, and an additional 230 young people who were inaccessible to interviewers filled out mail questionnaire forms of the instrument. The data base that will be employed for the rest of this book is the subsample of 676 women who were interviewed in both 1965 and 1973.[8] Only the female subsample is used for two reasons. First, as discussed above, the primary concern of this study is with the interrelationships of women's roles and not with sex differences. Second, although it is, of course, equally possible to examine the interrelationships among male roles, that would require extensive treatment of the theoretical issues concerning male roles, which is not the concern of this book. In addition, empirical analysis of male roles that would be analogous to that performed here for women would require indicators that are not available in this survey.[9] Male responses to the questions used here will be reported from time to time for descriptive purposes (N=672).

These data provide a unique opportunity to study the effects of women's private roles on their political involvement for four reasons. First, the availability of panel data permits the use of earlier responses to questions as a baseline by which to judge the effects of adult roles on attitudes and behavior. Second, the women in the sample were in their mid-twenties in 1973; thus there was considerable variation in their private roles. We will compare mothers and childless women, single and married women, homemakers and employed women, as well as the various combinations among these. Third, because the women are all approximately the same age, one can examine the effects of different roles without becoming entangled in the problems of comparing women of different generations at the same time.

Perhaps the most intriguing feature of these data is the particular generation represented in this sample. These women finished high school in 1965, just before the women's movement days, at a time when changes in the status and roles of women had already begun. Employment of women was on the rise. Women and men were beginning to gain college educations in equal proportions. Congress had just passed the 1964 Civil Rights Act, which included Title VII, making discrimination against women in employment illegal. The Supreme Court was declaring in *Griswold* v. *Connecticut* (1965) that married women have a constitutional right to practice birth control. The women in the sample who went to college were graduated during or after 1969, when the Women's Liberation Movement was gaining widespread attention, especially on college campuses. By the time the second wave of interviews took place in 1973, the women's movement was firmly established, the Equal Rights Amendment had been proposed by Congress, and the ratification process had been set in motion. This cohort was one of the first to take up its adult roles after the initial development of the Women's Liberation Movement, during one of the most important eras in the history of women.

This sample, therefore, does not represent a cross section of the American female population. The findings cannot be generalized to the present female population as a whole. It represents a unique and important subgroup: the new, post–women's movement generation of adults. This generation of women has more choices open to it than did any previous generation of women. This study investigates the political consequences of those choices. These women represent the new "average women," women who, by and large, continue to get married and have children, but who also take up careers. Their children will not remember the time when only a minority of women worked outside the home. They may not remember a time when the number of women in the House of Representatives couldn't fill one Congressional ladies room.

The methods employed here represent an attempt to redress some of the problems of role analysis mentioned above. As far as private gender roles go, it is impossible here to provide variables that are more sensitive to role structure variations than are available through check-off categories such as "married," "employed," and so on. A greater amount of precision is gained, however, through direct investigation of "privatization," the women's acceptance or rejection of the norm that "women's place is in the home." Thus, we will analyze a measure of role ideology that is distinct from the identification of the roles themselves. Each of these variables is discussed more completely below.

In an effort to determine the relative impact of different aspects of women's private roles on their political orientations and behavior, the predominant statistical treatment of the data is multiple regression. This technique allows us to examine the relative effects of multiple roles such as motherhood and homemaking on political involvement, as well as to assess the total amount of variance in women's political involvement accounted for by women's private roles when considered together. There will be times when the analysis reported here will seem to contradict other studies when, in truth, that is not the case. By using multiple regression we are looking for the direct and relative effects of specific roles. Thus, for example, when Chapter 6 shows no relationship between employment and political participation, that does not mean that employed women are not more participative than are homemakers. In fact, at the zero-order, they are. What the analysis does mean is that there is no significant *direct* relationship between the two. This technique, then, is a relatively conservative one; it makes more demands on the data before it will tell us there is "something there" than would be true using some other approaches.[10]

One additional aspect of the statistical analysis should be noted. As discussed earlier, the intention of this study is to isolate the effects of *adult* roles and ideology on political roles. This task would be particularly difficult if we only had access to data from one time point. If, for example, we found an inverse relationship between

being a homemaker and political participation, as many have speculated we should, two conclusions could be drawn. One is that being
a homemaker inhibits participation, the other is that nonparticipa-
tive women are particularly likely to choose homemaking as a
career. Access to panel data, or a study that "looks in on" the same
group of people more than once, alleviates this problem. In this
data set the respondents were asked many of the same questions
in 1965, before they had left high school, and in 1973, when they
had at least begun to assume adult roles. By entering the 1965
responses into the regression equations along with the other independent variables, we gain a clearer estimation of the effects of adult
roles. We will know whether the later attitudes and behavior are
at all functions of things that have happened to the women since
high school.

Education

Education is perhaps the most commonly used variable in social
research and will be used both as an independent variable and, from
time to time, as a "control" in this study. It is an important indicator of socio-economic status and cognitive training. More specifically relevant here, education loosely defines subcultures with different gender role conceptions. Changes in traditional gender role
norms occur first among the educated stratum and then diffuse
throughout society.[11] Also, education itself is still more highly valued
for males than females, although males and females are now
graduated from high schools and colleges in roughly equivalent
numbers.

For many years social scientists have been trying to discover the
effects of a college education on personality, perceptions, and values.
One of the most famous is the "Bennington Study," a survey of students from 1935–39 at Bennington College, a women's school in
Vermont.[12] One of the major findings of that study was a trend
toward first, an increase in interest in politics and second, an increase
in political and economic liberalism as the women progressed
through their college careers. In a follow-up study done twenty years
later, Newcomb and his associates found that the changes which
occurred while these women were in college were lasting ones for
the most part.

Another study, by James Trent and Leland Medsker,[13] analyzed changes in men and women over a four-year period following graduation from high school. They found that those who went to college increased significantly in levels of reflective thinking and tolerance for ambiguity and intellectual inquiry. The same was true for reflective thinking among men who were employed immediately after college. Women who went directly from high school to a job decreased in levels of toleration of ambiguity, and those who became homemakers "fell back" on both toleration of ambiguity and reflective thinking. College-educated women and men became less authoritarian, which was not true for people of either sex who were employed right after high school or for women who became homemakers. Education is also positively correlated with a number of political variables, including interest, efficacy, trust, activity and liberalism.

These effects of education have major implications for gender roles. Women were traditionally more conservative than men, less interested and active in politics, less efficacious, and more parochial.[14] Thus, many of the often noted differences between men and women may have been the results of differential access to education.[15] Moreover, higher education is associated with increased egalitarian attitudes toward the sexes and later entry into marriage and parenthood.[16] In turn, gender egalitarianism is related to nonauthoritarianism and liberalism.[17] The trend toward higher education of women may dramatically alter their political roles.

If students' political perceptions and orientations are measurably altered not only by a college education but by the general college experience, as the Bennington researchers indicated, the college-educated women in this study are sure to have been affected by the events of the late 1960s, including the women's movement. The years following 1965 were the active "late '60s," when the peace movement, black power groups, and various other student movements received a large amount of press for their campus actions. Even those who entered college immediately after high school were certainly present at the creation of the Women's Liberation Movement.

Forty-six percent of the women in this study had no schooling after high school graduation, 25 percent had some college education, and 28 percent were graduated from college. The women who went to college felt the profound effect of higher education on their lives; over half of the college-educated women (55 percent) reported that some aspect of their college experience challenged some "important beliefs or values" they had previously held.[18] In response to a follow-up probe,[19] the largest number of women mentioned moral issues (59 percent), particularly religion. Many of the changes also concerned political matters (18 percent) or general personal changes (13 percent). The vast majority of those who indicated that they were challenged claimed to have experienced changes in themselves, usually saying they became more liberal, more tolerant, or less traditional. Throughout the analysis the variable, "education" will refer to whether or not the woman has at least some college education (1 = no college education, 2 = at least some college education).

Marriage

At one time most girls were taught that their adult lives would be set as soon as they got married and began a family. Once married, a woman's husband and home, and, eventually, her children, were the focal point of her life until "death do them part." Much has been said about the decline of the family, but we have little indication that marriage as such has fallen from favor in recent years. It is true that the average age at first marriage has been rising since the middle of the 1950s, the divorce rate has been increasing during the same period, the number of women reporting themselves as cohabiting with a man without the blessing of church or state is rising, and the activism of lesbian feminists in the 1970s has relieved many women of the social necessity of staying within relationships that are contradictory to their own preferences. On the other hand, it is also clear that large numbers of women simply marry at a later age than did their mothers; they are not necessarily rejecting marriage. The vast number of remarriages shows that while a substantial portion of the population feels freer to reject a particular marriage, they do not necessarily reject the institution. The average woman gets married more often than she ever did before.

Studies of women and the family show that marital status may have important political implications. First, marriage has at least three different status-related meanings for women. A woman who becomes a wife gains communal, legal, and often theological recognition that she has become a new person. Traditionally the woman, unlike the man, gains a new title and a new name. As Helen Lopata puts it, the radical change in her persona is "symbolized by dropping her former identity in title and group name. . . . The man's identity remains unchanged, as far as his symbolic title and name are concerned."[20] Until relatively recently, the law liquidated a woman as a distinct person upon marriage.

Another crucial aspect of marriage concerns status acquisition. Women acquire a socio-economic status through marriage more easily than is true for men. A married woman's socio-economic status is judged by her husband's occupation and not by her own, even when she is employed, but particularly when she is not. Harriet Holter suggests that because recruitment to marital roles and female adult identity is based in principle on ascribed status rather than achieved status, ascription has a greater impact on women's identities and values than on men's. Hence, she argues that women are more inclined to respect and defer to ascribed status and existing social structure than men in general. She sees this deference to ascription as one basis for women's conservatism.[21] Questioning or rejecting the authority of marriage has been, quite simply, more dangerous for women than for men.

We must add to this list of the meanings of marriage for women in politics the norms of dependence. It is true that women have more freedom of choice to enter and leave marriages than they ever had before, and that the *ideal* of the "companionate" marriage is widespread. At the same time, however, law and social custom still maintain the husband as the head of the household in a number of respects.[22] Especially for the homemaker, a married woman remains dependent to a large degree on the husband for psychological and economic support.[23] To the degree that individual women are dependent upon their husbands, they must entrust final authority to them in order to remain secure in their positions and not be rejected. Norms of dependence have implications for a variety of situations, including political, outside the narrow confines of women's private roles.[24]

A majority (72 percent) of the women in the sample are married. One quarter of the college-educated women were never married as opposed to only 11 percent of the high school graduates. This is consistent with what we would expect, of course, because college-educated women generally marry later (Table 4:1). Throughout the analysis the variable, "marriage" will refer to whether or not the woman is married and living with her husband. (1=not currently married, including separated, 2=married.)

Table 4:1
Marital Status, by Education

Marital Status	No College (%)	College (%)
Married	79	66
Cohabit	0	3
Widowed	1	0
Separated, Divorced	9	6
Never Married	11	25
Total	100	100
(N)	(286)	(389)

Motherhood

By far the greater number of family relevant hypotheses concerning female political roles revolve around motherhood rather than wifehood. Motherhood has been seen as the source of relatively low levels of political involvement, except perhaps at the local level, as the reason for low levels of political efficacy, and as the motivation for particular interest in family-oriented, social welfare, and peace issues.[25]

About 42 percent of the women in this study are mothers. Twenty-one percent have one child, 17 percent have two, and almost 5 percent have three or more. Sixty-one percent have children only under the age of five, 28 percent have at least one child under the age of five and at least one of school age, and 12 percent have children only of school age. For most of the women in this study, "motherhood" means responsibility for preschoolers. Not all of the women who have children are married; nearly 13 percent of them are not. For these women we should expect even greater constraints of motherhood.

A higher proportion of the respondents with only a high school education are mothers regardless of marital status. Table 4:2 shows the relationships among marital status and motherhood controlling for education. These figures underscore the problem of single motherhood. The high school graduates marry younger, have children at a younger age, and are more likely to end up as single mothers at a young age. They are also less likely to have the financial resources or earning potential to deal with this burden. Throughout the analysis the variable, "motherhood," will refer to whether or not the woman has any children (1=no children, 2=children).

Table 4:2
Age of Youngest Child, by Education and Marital Status

Age of Child	No College		College	
	Married (%)	Single (%)	Married (%)	Single (%)
No Children	27	64	57	91
Child ≤ 5 years	69	27	42	6
Child ≥ 6 years	5	9	0	3
Total	101[a]	100	99[a]	100
(N)	(200)	(55)	(234)	(132)

[a]Column does not add to 100% because of rounding error.

Homemaking

Almost half of adult American women do not have an occupation in the traditional sense — they are housewives. The housewife provides many problems for the social analyst. Her occupation is not included in scales measuring social status of occupations and is not even considered an occupation by many people, yet she is also not considered unemployed. A housewife is simply not in the employment pool. This is not to say that the role of the married employed female is simply defined, either. Most often when one wishes to measure a woman's social status, one uses her father's or husband's occupation, regardless of her own employment status. Moreover, despite her occupational commitments, a married employed woman continues to fill the homemaking role as well.

Homemaking is an occupation. It is a job that requires some amount of training; it has particular duties, usually including cooking, cleaning, counseling, and often childcare. It is a means of financial support. Helen Lopata, in her book, *Occupation: Housewife*, summed up the argument for considering housewife as an occupational category as follows: "[What] kind of role could it [housewife] be, if not an occupational one? All family roles are located within a kinship organizational structure, but it clearly has no place on the family tree. It can be performed by a widow with no children or other family members who directly benefit from it. Only humorists label it as a recreational role. The counterpart male role is always a specific occupation."[26] By law, it is homemaking that, in large part, serves as the basis of a woman's right to support from her husband.

As discussed earlier, most discussions of roles and role conflicts among women center on the problem of occupation. In the preceding chapter the discussion of roles pointed out the low salience of employment in women's role sets. Most laws barring women from combining employment roles with the maternal are gone, but a relatively traditional role set remains. In the 1974 Virginia Slims Poll[27] women were asked what combination of the statuses of marriage, motherhood and career would offer "the most satisfying and interesting life." Fifty-two percent of the women surveyed chose all three together, while 38 percent chose only marrying and having children. The young and highly educated were even more likely to choose the combination of roles. Very few imagined a career without having children.

The complex problem which remains, then, is that no matter how many women actually are employed, the dominant roles — even among employed women — are those in the home. As the results of the Virginia Slims Poll indicate, the vast majority of American women cannot imagine themselves happy without both marriage and children; 39 percent of the women felt the most satisfying life would not include a career. Cynthia Fuchs Epstein has pointed out the impact of the traditional role hierarchy among working women. As she wrote, "The married, middle class woman who works does not live a day without the knowledge that she can choose not to work and that on balance, a decision to give up working probably will meet with more social support and approval than any arrangement she may have worked out to harmonize her work and home life."[28]

Homemaking has often been held responsible for women's low levels of participation and what are seen as parochial issue stands. The homemaker is also the woman who most closely approximates cultural expectations made of women, and therefore is expected also to perform in the political system in stereotyped ways.

For purposes of empirical analysis, a housewife is a married woman who calls herself a housewife when she is asked about her occupation. Women who say they are employed, unemployed, laid off, or looking for work are in the workforce.[29] (The variable, "homemaking," is coded 1=in the workforce, 2=homemaker.) This distinction between "housewife" and "unemployed" is made because these answers indicate different role definitions; the latter woman considers herself in the workforce while the former does not.

The college-educated women are less likely than the high school graduates to be married and are more likely to be in the workforce (Table 4:3). Married women with children are, of course, more likely to be housewives than those who are not mothers (Table 4:4). We cannot know whether these women will return to work when their children are older, although it appears likely that many will. Among these women 60 percent of the women with pre–school-aged children are homemakers compared with 21 percent of the women whose children are all at least five years old.

Table 4:3
Marital and Employment Status,
by Education

Status	No College (%)	College (%)
Housewife	43	21
Married, In Workforce	38	44
Single, In Workforce	19	34
Total	100	99[a]
(N)	(280)	(389)

[a]Column does not add to 100% because of rounding error.

Table 4:4
Employment Status, by Education and Marital Status

	No College		College	
Status	No Children (%)	Children (%)	No Children (%)	Children (%)
Housewife	17	65	8	57
In Workforce	83	35	93	43
Total	100	100	101[a]	100
(N)	(53)	(147)	(134)	(100)

[a]Column does not add to 100% because of rounding error.

To describe briefly the types of jobs these women hold, the largest occupational category for college-educated women is professional or business (Table 4:5). Among those who are in the workforce, over half of the college-educated women have professional and business jobs; over half the high school graduates are lower status white collar workers.[30] There are no significant differences between married and single women or between mothers and nonmothers.

Table 4:5
Occupation, by Education

Occupation	No College (%)		College (%)	
Professional-Business	7	(13)[a]	43	(55)
White Collar	31	(54)	30	(38)
Blue Collar	19	(33)	5	(7)
Housewife	43	–	22	–
Total	100	100	100	100
(N)	(279)		(370)	

[a]Column in parentheses shows the distribution of occupations only among women in the workforce.

Privatization

One of the themes in the first three chapters was privatization, the concept that exposes the domination of women's lives by private roles, concerns, and values. Even where women are involved in public life, as in the workforce and politics, their activities and concerns are expected to be imbued with the private significance of being a woman. This is what we mean by "privatization."[31]

There need not be a one-to-one correspondence of women's own ideology and the actual activities in which women are engaged. Many women are employed outside the home because there is no other way for their families to survive; they do not necessarily have a "liberated" understanding of women's roles and may, in fact, look forward to the day when they can "go home." Homemakers, on the other hand, may be intensely involved in public issues and activities. Many women in public office list their occupation as "housewife." It is also true that women can become involved in politics and remain privatized in a sense. These women become involved in issues that directly concern their families, often through organizations such as the PTA, and may continue to *interpret* their political activities as part of their roles as homemakers and mothers.

The variable here labelled "privatization" taps very directly women's understanding of women as public or private creatures. The women were asked to position themselves on a continuum that ranged from "women and men should have an equal role [in business, industry, and government]" to "women's place is in the home."[32] Table 4:6 shows the relationship between privatization and the variables discussed earlier. The first notable feature of the analysis is that there is certainly a relationship between privatization and role structures plus education, but it is not nearly as strong as some might expect: only 14 percent of the variance is explained by these variables together in the total sample. In the total sample of women, education and homemaking are significantly related to privatization. Examining the same relationships at the zero order, 34 percent of the high school graduates and 60 percent of those with some college education scored low on privatization. The importance of higher education as a shaper of women's gender role ideology is highlighted by examining the relationship between privatization and the college-educated women's perceptions of college as an experience that challenged their basic beliefs. Fifty percent of those who did not feel so challenged by college scored low on privatization, compared with 72 percent of those who did. Although few of the women directly mentioned gender roles as part of their changes, it is clear that higher education may be one of the most important agents of change in women's roles and understanding of themselves.

Table 4:6
Determinants of Privatization, by Education

Determinants	Total	No College	College
Education	−.21*	—	—
Marriage	.04	.09	.00
Motherhood	.06	−.06	.17*
Homemaking	.19*	.21*	.17*
R^2	.14	.06	.09
(N)	(607)	(251)	(356)

Note. Unless specified otherwise, entries are standardized regression coefficients and data are drawn from the 1973 wave of the survey throughout this chapter.
*$p < .05$.

Women who are homemakers are more privatized than are those who are in the labor force. The homemaker's occupation is centered on the home, and they are more likely to interpret women's roles as revolving around the home. Eight percent of the women in the workforce scored high on privatization compared with 26 percent of the homemakers. It is important to note, however, that the relationship is not necessarily as strong as many feminists' assertions might lead us to believe. Motherhood does not bear the same relationship to privatization in the two educational groups. While there is no significant relationship among the high school graduates, college-educated women without children are less privatized than are college-educated mothers.

Feminism

Thus far little has been said of feminism. The rejection of privatization is certainly part of feminism, but only part. There are feminists who are married and those who are single, feminists who are mothers and those who have no children, feminists who are employed and those who are homemakers.

Although one would be hard pressed to imagine a woman who believes a "woman's place is in the home" as a feminist, the basic egalitarianism expressed by those who believe that "women should have equal roles" in the public sector is a necessary but not sufficient condition for calling someone a feminist. The issue of what constitutes feminism has been dealt with extensively elsewhere, but a brief discussion here will clarify the author's assumptions in this volume.[33]

Definitions of feminism vary considerably. There are certain elements in common, however, that can be outlined here as a basic set of components of feminism. First, feminists believe that women should be freer to make choices about their "life options."[34] Some feminists feel that the goal of feminism is concerned primarily with giving women equal opportunities with those of men.[35] This aspect of feminism requires a rejection of privatization.

It is possible for one to believe that women and men should have equal opportunities but also to believe that these opportunities are currently available. Although feminism does not require a Ph.D. in women's studies, it does require some variation of what is called "feminist consciousness," an ability to free oneself enough of the official ideology of equality or role complementarity in order to understand the ways in which women have been constrained, to understand the ways in which women need liberation. Women still have relatively little control over their own lives; they have considerably less influence in the important institutions in society including, especially, government.

The women in this study were asked whether women have "too much influence" in American society and politics, "just about the right amount of influence," or "too little influence." As Table 4:7 shows, analysis of the responses to this question reveals that women who reject the norm of privatization are more likely to feel that women have less influence than men than do those who say that woman's place is in the home. College education has a similar effect on the women's perceptions of female influence. Even employment, which one might think would make women more aware of the problems of women, has no significant bearing on this perception.

Table 4:7
Determinants of Perceiving Women as
Having Too Little Influence

Determinants	
Education	.10*
Marriage	−.07
Motherhood	.00
Homemaking	−.03
Privatization	−.43*
R^2	.23
(N)	(564)

Note. For further explanation see Table 4:6.
*$p < .05$.

Although privatization is clearly related to the women's perceptions of women's influence, this relationship is not as strong as one might suspect. About 30 percent of the women who felt that men's and women's responsibilities in society should be equal also felt that women have about the right amount of power now. About 19 percent of those who basically believe that women should stay at home also feel that women have too little power. This latter set of attitudes has emerged a number of times in history. Many reformers of the late nineteenth and early twentieth centuries serve as examples. They felt that women should be wives and mothers primarily, but that an increase in women's influence would bring morality and nurturance into politics.

Feminism entails an attitude that women's roles should be expanded as well as a "feminist consciousness," the ability to see the ways in which women's lives are currently limited. It also requires that one believe in the necessity of group action, especially on the part of women, to achieve desired changes. Exactly what type of group and what type of action varies considerably across the spectrum of feminism. Feminist strategies range from traditional lobbying techniques to community organizing to provide social services such as day care or shelters for battered wives to self-help consciousness-raising groups to separatist women's organizations. Most feminists would agree, however, that profession of egalitarianism, or even a perception of specific women's problems, is not sufficient; feminism also includes a belief in group action for social change.

This survey included one question that could be used to get a handle on the women's feelings about group efforts for change. They were asked for their attitudes toward the Women's Liberation Movement, a catch-all label including the varieties of feminism current in the late 1960s and early 1970s. Though never, as the mass media tried to define it, a cohesive organization with a clear set of leaders and a programme, the women's attitudes toward the Movement would reflect their attitude toward organizations of women acting for change in women's roles.

The question included in this survey called for the women to express their feelings toward the Women's Liberation Movement as "cold," "neutral," or "warm."[36] Eighteen percent of the responses fell on the cold side of the measure, 49 percent were neutral, and 34 percent were warm. Education makes a considerable difference in the women's evaluation of the Movement; 21 percent of the high school graduates felt warm compared with 44 percent of the college-educated women. This educational difference makes sense for two reasons. First, as we have seen, higher education promoted gender egalitarianism and, to the degree that this is one of the goals of the women's movement, should also promote positive attitudes toward the Movement. The women who felt challenged in their basic beliefs by their college education were even more favorable toward the Movement; 35 percent of those who did not feel challenged were favorable compared with 55 percent of those who did.

The second reason for the connection between college education and attitudes toward the women's movement concerns the locus of its original development. Much of the initial organizing took place on college campuses at about the time when these women were in college. Thus the college-educated women undoubtedly had more contact with the movement than did the women who were not in school. The latter group probably had little more contact than that provided by the predominantly negative images provided by the mass media.[37]

Because of the very different contact experienced by the two different educational groups, the multivariate analysis of attitudes toward the Women's Liberation Movement is displayed for the two groups separately in Table 4:8. The sources of attitudes toward the feminist movement differ slightly for the two groups. The clearest difference is in the negative effect of marriage among the high school graduates as compared with the lack of any relationship among the college educated. At the zero-order level, 15 percent of the married and 42 percent of the single high school graduates felt warm toward the movement. The same was true of 39 percent of the married and 50 percent of the single college-educated women. We may assume that the difference in the direct relationship is due at least in part to the type of contact with feminism experienced by the women. At that time, the media tended to present feminists as a wild group of women who disliked men and liked to burn their underwear.[38] No doubt the married women whose only contact was via that image felt extremely threatened. In this respect it is important to note that the level of education makes considerably more difference among married than among single women.

Table 4:8

Determinants of Warm Feelings toward the
Women's Liberation Movement, by Education

Predictors	No College	College
Marriage	−.20*	−.03
Motherhood	.00	.02
Homemaking	.06	−.02
Privatization	−.32*	−.49*
Too Little Influence	.21*	.20*
R²	.26	.37
(N)	(235)	(326)

Note. For further explanation see Table 4:6.
*p < .05.

Another difference between the high school graduates and the college-educated women is the difference in the translation of a belief in equality into support for the movement. This "translation" appears to be somewhat more strong among the college-educated women. Once again, this difference may be attributed to the different types of contact the women had with feminists. In other respects the sources of attitudes toward the women's movement appears to be the same for high school graduates and college-educated women. Neither maternal nor employment status has any direct effect on feelings toward the movement. Among both groups those who feel women have too little influence in society are more likely to feel warm toward the movement, although this relationship is not as strong as one might expect.

This analysis of the components of feminism should highlight one major point: this book is not, strictly speaking, an analysis of the effects of feminism on women's political roles.[39] Change in roles, private and public, is certainly the goal of feminism. Further, these women have political opportunities that were not available to past generations. For now we will be considering political involvement that includes feminists, nonfeminists, and antifeminists. The irony, of course, is that the opportunities won for women by feminists of one generation provide increased opportunities for the antifeminists of the next generation. We will return to the question of feminism as such and its relationship to political integration in the Conclusion.

Summary

We have now developed both micro- and macro-level frameworks within which to assess the degree of female integration into the American political system at the mass level. Because of the melange of hypotheses, findings, myths, and stereotypes commonly presented as descriptions of women's relationship to politics, each of the independent variables discussed here (education, marriage, motherhood, homemaking, and privatization) will be examined for its effects on each aspect of women's political roles discussed in the course of analysis. It should not, therefore, be expected that each independent variable is significantly associated with each dependent variable. Indeed, it would be surprising if they were. Rather, by piecing together the various connections and disconnections between the different facets of private roles and political roles we should gain a clearer picture of the web we call political integration.

NOTES

1. For more discussion of the meanings of masculinity and femininity, see Ann Constantinople, "Masculinity-Femininity: An Exception to a Famous Dictum?" *Psychological Bulletin* 80 (1973), 389-407; Sandra Bem, "The Measurement of Psychological Androgyny," *Journal of Consulting and Clinical Psychology* 42 (1974), 155-62; Janet T. Spence, Robert Helmreich, and J. Stapp, "Ratings of Self and Peers on Sex Role Attributes and Their Relation to Self-Esteem and Conceptions of Masculinity and Femininity," *Journal of Personality and Social Psychology* 32 (1975), 29-39; David Tresemer, "Assumptions Made about Gender Roles," In Marcia Millman and Rosabeth Moss Kanter, eds., *Another Voice* (Garden City: Doubleday, 1975), pp. 308-39.
2. On sexist biases in political science, see Susan Bourke and Jean Grossholtz, "Politics as an Unnatural Practice: Political Science Looks at Female Participation," *Politics and Society* (Winter, 1974), 255-66; Murray Goot and Elizabeth Reid, "Women and Voting Studies: Mindless Matrons or Sexist Scientism?" (Beverly Hills: Sage Professional Papers in Contemporary Political Sociology, 1975); Jan Morgan, "Women and Political Socialization: Fact and Fantasy in Easton and Dennis and in Lane," *Politics* 9 (May, 1975), 50-55; Goldie Shabad and Kristi Andersen, "Candidate Evaluations by Men and Women," *Public Opinion Quarterly* 43 (Spring, 1979), 18-35; Virginia Sapiro, "Women's Studies and Political Conflict," in Julia Sherman and Evelyn Beck., ed., *The Prism of Sex: Essays in the Sociology of Knowledge* (Madison: University of Wisconsin Press, 1979), pp. 253-65.
3. Robert Lane, *Political Life* (New York: Macmillan, 1959).
4. Robert Dahl, *Who Governs?* (New Haven: Yale University Press, 1961), p. 156. For more discussion of the treatment of women in *Who Governs?* see Sapiro, "Women's Studies and Political Conflict."
5. Fred I. Greenstein, *Children and Politics* (New Haven: Yale University Press, 1969), Chapter VI.
6. Naomi B. Lynn and Cornelia B. Flora, "Motherhood and Political Participation: The Changing Sense of Self," *Journal of Political and Military Sociology* 1 (Spring, 1973), 91-103.
7. Lane, *Political Life.*
8. The second wave was run by the Center for Political Studies of the University of Michigan. For complete information on the study design, see the major works written by the primary investigators, M. Kent Jennings and Richard G. Niemi, *The Political Character of Adolescence* (Princeton: Princeton University Press, 1974) and Jennings and Niemi, *Generations and Politics: Young Adults and Their Parents* (Prince-

ton: Princeton University Press, 1981). The data and documentation are available from the archives of the Interuniversity Consortium for Political and Social Research, University of Michigan, Ann Arbor.

9. For male roles, see Warren Farrell, *The Liberated Man: Freeing Men and Their Relationships with Women* (New York: Random House, 1974); Marc Fasteau, *The Male Machine* (New York: McGraw Hill, 1974); Leonard Benson, *Fatherhood: A Sociological Perspective* (New York: Random House, 1967); Mirra Komarovsky, *Dilemmas of Masculinity: A Study of College Youth* (New York: Norton, 1976); Joseph Pleck and Jack Sawyer, eds., *Men and Masculinity* (Englewood Cliffs: Prentice-Hall, 1974); Andrew Tolson, *The Limits of Masculinity: Male Identity and Women's Liberation* (New York: Harper and Row, 1977). From the point of view of a feminist scholar it is interesting to note that when anyone's gender roles are considered in need of explanation, it is the woman's. We have heard of the "woman problem" or "woman question." What about the "man problem" or "man question"?

10. This analysis involves using a standard mathematical equation of the form:

$$Y = a + b_1X_1 + b_2X_2 + b_3X_3 \ldots$$

where Y is the dependent variable, such as political participation, which is to be explained with reference to the independent variables (X_1, X_2, X_3) such as marital and employment status and privatization. In fact, the most common equation used here will involve six predictors or determinants (independent variables, labeled "X"), including the 1965 score on the variable to be predicted, the level of education the respondent received by 1973, the respondent's marital, maternal, and employment status in 1973, and her response to the question of privatization in 1973. Using the example of political participation as the dependent (Y) variable, what we are asking, in effect, is, what is the weight of each of the independent variables in determining the degree to which a woman participates? Is her level of participation as an adult in 1973 "merely" a function of her childhood socialization and earlier participatory tendencies (represented by the 1965 participation score) and/or her level of education, or do her adult gender roles (marital, maternal, and employment status) or her gender ideology (privatization) affect her participation levels as well? For an introduction to social science methods that requires no background in statistics, see Fred Kerlinger, *Behavioral Research: A Conceptual Approach* (New York: Holt, Rinehart, and Winston, 1979).

11. Change in norms have occurred in most sectors of society, but looking at the various opinion studies over time shows higher-educated people consistently more egalitarian.

12. Theodore Newcomb et al., *Persistence and Change* (New York: Wiley, 1967).

13. James W. Trent and Leland L. Medsker, *Beyond High School* (San Francisco: Jossey-Bass, 1969), pp. 128-77.

14. Harriet Holter, *Sex Roles and Social Structure* (Oslo: Universitets-forlaget, 1970), *passim.*
15. For example, Sidney Verba, Norman Nie, and Jae-on Kim, *Participation and Political Equality: A Seven Nation Comparison* (Cambridge: Cambridge University Press, 1978).
16. Alice Eagly and Pamela Anderson, "Sex Roles and Attitudinal Correlates of Family Size," *Journal of Applied Social Psychology* 4 (1974), 151-64; Carol Tavris, "Who Likes Women's Liberation and Why," *Journal of Social Issues* 29 (1973), 175-98; Frank Clarkson et al., "Family Size and Sex Role Stereotypes," *Science* 167 (1970), 390-92; Abbot Ferriss, *Indicators of Trends in the Status of American Women* (New York: Russell Sage, 1971).
17. Tavris, "Who Likes Women's Liberation?"; Theodore Adorno et al., *The Authoritarian Personality* (New York: Norton, 1950), *passim.*
18. "When you were in college did you have any of your important beliefs challenged by fellow students, a professor, something you read, or something that happened?"
19. The respondents were allowed multiple responses. Only the first is used here.
20. Helen Lopata, *Occupation: Housewife* (New York: Oxford, 1971), p. 81.
21. Holter, *Sex Roles and Social Structure*, pp. 230-31.
22. For an excellent overview of the definitions of marriage in the legal system, see Barbara A. Brown, Ann E. Freedman, Harriet N. Katz, and Alice M. Price, *Women's Rights and the Law* (New York: Praeger, 1977).
23. For a discussion of the sociological dimensions of marriage, see Jessie Bernard, *The Future of Marriage* (New York: Bantam, 1972).
24. See Virginia Sapiro, "Sex and Games: On Oppression and Rationality," *British Journal of Political Science* 9 (Oct., 1979), 385-408.
25. Naomi B. Lynn and Cornelia B. Flora, "Motherhood and Political Participation: The Changing Sense of Self," *Journal of Political and Military Sociology* 1 (Spring, 1973), 91-103, and Goot and Reid, "Women and Voting Studies."
26. Lopata, *Occupation: Housewife*, p. 1391.
27. Roper Organization, *The Virginia Slims American Woman's Poll* (Roper Organization, 1974), p. 28.
28. Cynthia Fuchs Epstein, *Woman's Place* (Berkeley: University of California Press, 1970), p. 28.
29. Of those in the workforce, 90 percent are currently employed, 7 percent are laid off, looking for work, or unemployed, and 3 percent are students.
30. The occupational categories were formed by collapsing the U.S. census classifications. The first category consists of professional, semiprofessional, and managerial classifications; the second includes clerical and sales workers; the third includes all other blue collar occupations; the last includes housewives.

31. "Privatization" is more fully defined in Chapter 2.
32. "Recently there's been a lot of talk about women's rights. Some people feel that women should have an equal role with men in running business, industry, and government. Others feel that women's place is in the home. Where would you put yourself on this scale . . .?" A seven point scale, trichotomized as follows: Low = 1-2, medium = 3-5, high = 6-7.
33. In this treatment I am discussing only generally agreed upon principles of feminism, not a particular feminist philosophy. For analysis of feminist theories, see Sarah Slavin Schramm, *Plow Women Rather Than Reapers: An Intellectual History of Feminism in the United States* (Metuchen, N.J.: Scarecrow Press, 1979); Alison Jaggar, "Political Philosophies of Women's Liberation," in Mary Vetterling-Braggin et al., eds., *Feminism and Philosophy* (Totowa, N.J.: Littlefield, Adams, 1977), pp. 5-21; Sandra Lee Bartky, "Toward a Phenomenology of Feminist Consciousness," in Vetterling-Braggin, *Feminism and Philosophy*, pp. 22-34; Lynda M. Glennon, *Women and Dualism: A Sociology of Knowledge Analysis* (New York: Longman, 1979); Claire Fulenwider, *Feminism in American Politics* (New York: Praeger, 1980); Editors of *Quest, Building Feminist Theory* (New York: Longman, 1981).
34. "Life options" is taken from Janet Zollinger Giele, "Introduction: The Status of Women in Comparative Perspective," in Janet Giele and Audrey Chapman Smock, eds., *Women: Roles and Status in Eight Countries* (New York: Wiley, 1977), pp. 1-32.
35. I say "some" because many feminists reject the current structure of men's lives and opportunities as well. For a discussion of the problems of "equality" in feminist theory, see Schramm, *Plow Women Rather Than Reapers*, pp. 186-230.
36. The feeling thermometer is an instrument by which an affective response toward an object is ascertained. Respondents are asked to indicate the degree of warmth they feel, where 0° is the coldest, 50° neutral, and 100° the warmest. The responses were trichotomized so that the categories are 0°-39°, 40°-60°, and 61°-100° in order to preserve the relative purity of the extremes rather than the middle. The mean of the full scale falls within the neutral category of the collapsed scale.
37. For the history of the rise of the women's movement, see Judith Hole and Ellen Levine, *Rebirth of Feminism* (New York: Quadrangle, 1971); Jo Freeman, *The Politics of Women's Liberation* (New York: Longman, 1974); and Sara Evans, *Personal Politics: The Roots of Women's Liberation in the Civil Rights Movement and the New Left* (New York: Random House, 1979).
38. On the treatment of women and the women's movement in the mass media, see Gaye Tuchman, Arlene Kaplan Daniels, and James Benet, eds., *Hearth and Home: Images of Women in the Mass Media* (New York: Oxford University Press, 1978).
39. That task is undertaken in Fulenwider, *Feminism in American Politics*.

CHAPTER 5

Political Involvement: Orientations, Motivations, and Resources

The process of political integration, as argued in Chapter 2, involves an alteration of "webs of significance," that is, change in individuals' understanding of and sense of relationship to the political system. In order to be a full-fledged citizen of a democratic polity, one must see at least some of the connections between government and politics and one's own life. But seeing "connections" is not enough; we are also interested in the types of connections people see and feel. We assume that the citizen, especially as compared with the subject, identifies with the system, has some knowledge of it, will feel obliged to support it in various fashions, but will also have a predilection to place demands on it through acts of participation. As Gabriel Almond and Sidney Verba note in their discussion of citizenship, "No zealous advocate of good citizenship would argue that political participation ought to be pursued to the neglect of all other obligations."[1] But, as they also say, a citizen's involvement must go beyond responding to the state's extractive rights and the individual's private concerns.[2] Political participation, and a predilection toward participation, are democratic values of citizenship in and of themselves.

In recent years women's political participation has been the subject of considerable discussion and research. One point that is often missing in these debates is definition of the value or functions of political participation. The way in which we define the values and functions of participation directly affects the way in which we will evaluate women's political activity and the goals we set for their activity.

If we review the various functions of participation, that is, the value of participation for the participant and the political system as a whole, we arrive at three views. The first, and most commonly mentioned in contemporary works on democratic theory is protection for the individual, especially as enunciated through discussions of representation and negotiation among competing interests.[3] This function, when analyzed to its logical conclusion, suggests some limits to democracy. If participation is, in effect, combat among pretenders to individual or even group interests, too much democratic participation can "overheat" a political system, causing political instability.[4] This conception of political participation logically leads to the conclusion that the only reason to take group demands for increased participation and influence seriously is that a group has a particular set of interests that is not but ought to be represented in political contests.

The second function of participation serves as a warning against blithe acceptance of the protection function. This is the function of ritual and the creation of acquiescence.[5] If one wishes to use the terms of systems theory, this second approach to participation reminds us that participation in politics does not simply place *demands* on a system; it also serves a *support* function; that is, it provides an important ballast for the political system. Thus through the late 1960s and into the 1970s the precipitous drop in trust in government and the decline of partisan identification coupled with what appeared to be "voter apathy" signaled for many commentators a crisis in American politics. The crisis was often discussed not so much in terms of the political problems that gave rise to changes in voter behavior, but in terms of changes in the voter's attitudes and behavior. Even the decline in trust and partisanship alone were not the primary sources of worry. The "crisis" was the apparent decline in a willingness to participate through regularized, acceptable, and relatively innocuous channels. Few people interpreted the 1970s decline in street protests and other forms of nonconventional participation as a crisis in democracy. This second approach to participation suggests that one must think about the psychological bases and modes of participation in order to understand the meaning of political participation for specified groups. There are circumstances under which participation may have precious little to do with demands, protection of interests, or representation. Participation may sometimes serve the same function for citizenship that touching one's toes three times once a week serves for physical health.

The third function of participation which, as Carole Pateman points out, is too often ignored in contemporary democratic theory, is that of political education. Participation is, in the words of many contemporary advertisements for children's toys, "learning by doing." Democratic participation may both depend on and foster particular sets of skills and psychological characteristics. As Pateman writes:

> . . . the belief that one can be self-governing, and confidence in one's ability to participate responsibly and effectively, and to control one's life and environment would certainly seem to be required. These are not characteristics that would be associated with "servile" or "passive" characters and it is reasonable to suggest that the acquisition of such confidence, etc., is part . . . of what the theorists of the participatory society saw as the psychological benefits that would accrue through participation.[6]

This confidence, self-esteem, or sense of efficacy should also be necessary as a basis for democratic participation.

Contemporary political scientists have run many computer tapes in the course of investigating the sources, distribution, and effects of psychological characteristics such as efficacy, trust, and interest. Most often these characteristics have been thought of as predispositions or motivations, as parts of the personality that help provide the "push" or reason for participation. These characteristics may appropriately be considered as "motivations" in part. The fact that I develop an interest in or sense of competence about politics may well give me the spur to act. In a large sense, however, these characteristics are mislabeled "motivations," especially for participation. I may be interested in football or theater, I may even feel I understand football or theater well, and that I could certainly give Fran Tarkenton, Woody Hayes, Lillian Hellman, or Lord Olivier a pointer or two. But this does not mean I have any motivation to play or coach football, write plays, or deliver a soliloquy. I may simply become an avid — but inactive — observer. The same is true of politics.

A number of people are beginning to think of these characteristics not as motivations but as resources. Although Pateman appears unaware of the distinction in her work, she indicates that the development of a sense of competence and other psychological results of participation in democratic organizations constitutes the learning of skills upon which a citizen may draw in political situations. More recently, Sidney Verba, Norman Nie, and Jae-on Kim discuss the psychological resources of political involvement that may be brought to bear on or be "converted into" political activity.[7] They describe political rights (of participation) as opportunities for participation open to citizens. But, as we have seen, rights confer opportunities in only a limited sense. Despite any legal guarantee of equal opportunity to participate, "If there are significant differences in resources and motivation, new participatory opportunities can mean more inequality in participation as those with the resources and motivation use the opportunities available to them."[8] Quite apart from the legal right to participate in politics, if psychological resources such as efficacy, trust, interest, or knowledge are disproportionately limited in certain social groups, so is the "net weight" likelihood of participation.

A discussion of psychological resources for participation in politics is crucial for understanding women's relationship to politics and government. As we saw earlier, the psychological resources of interest, knowledge, and efficacy are among the first aspects of political involvement in which males and females differ. Studies of adults also reveal sex differences in these "cognitive" and motivational resources. More to the point for our purposes, many of the norms of femininity are in direct conflict with those associated with the democratic participant. The ideals of docility, passivity, irrationality, dependence, and the resulting low levels of self-esteem found among women are more appropriate to the subject than to the citizen, or to the acquiescent semicitizen than to the full participant. The view that full citizens concern themselves with issues that go beyond immediate personal concerns also conflicts with traditional images of women.

The importance of psychological resources such as interest and efficacy for the study of women is underscored by the work of Verba, Nie, Kim, and Shabad. They attempted one of the first empirical investigations of the question of whether women (a) "abstain from politics because they do not care about political matters" or (b) "care about politics but are inhibited from participating because of external restraints or self-restraint."[9] They looked at socioeconomic resources (education), psychological involvement (interest and efficacy), and political activity (conventional). They found, as others have, that women scored lower than did men on all three variables in every country they studied; women have fewer socioeconomic resources, fewer psychological resources, and participate less. Verba and his colleagues did find, however, that women "convert" socio-economic resources into psychological involvement at about the same rate that men do. In further analysis, they found that women's involvement is not converted into actual activity at nearly the rate that is true for men. By these findings they show that part of what keeps women less involved in politics is their lack of access to socio-economic resources; but once they do become involved, that is, once they gain the psychological resources necessary for political participation, they are inhibited from using these for participation.

We shall consider the problem of participation specifically in Chapter 6. For now, there is a remaining problem concerning psychological resources. Women's gain in psychological resources is as great as is men's for every step up in education, but at each level of education women's involvement remains lower than in that of men.[10] Why is this the case? The relationships between women's private roles and participatory orientations may reveal part of the answer. A number of researchers have suggested that adult experiences, but in public and private organizations, may be very important in shaping participatory resources in politics.[11] We have also seen that the traditional norms of femininity and women's roles are contradictory to those we expect of fully active citizens. We will turn now to direct investigation of the relationship between women's private roles and psychological resources, including political interest, understanding, efficacy, trust and citizen duty.

Political Interest

One of the most universal observations of women's roles in politics is that they are not as interested in politics and public affairs as are men. This finding has been noted for both children and adults.[12] Not all of these studies use the same measure of interest; some use answers to direct questions about political interests, others use general questions about "following" politics, still others use responses to questions about how often the respondent discusses politics, and some use media usage. Sometimes these studies cannot be taken at face value because of the reflection of sex bias in them. Fred I. Greenstein, for example, demonstrates the relative lack of political interest in girls by citing studies that showed, "Neither sex dominated in the meager factual awareness of [World War II] at this age, but when asked which of a series of pictures they preferred, nine of the boys and *none* of the girls picked war pictures." He also cited evidence that boys were considerably more likely than girls to be "enthusiastic or excited" about the war.[13] Greenstein gives as an example of girls' "nonpolitical" responses the desire to "get rid of all the criminals and bad people."[14] Apparently, liking war is political while a desire for law and order is not. We can have little trust in some types of sex difference reporting.

The pervasiveness of childhood differences in political interest suggests that childhood socialization is responsible for links between gender and political interest, and that we should find little in the way of direct effects of adult roles. On the other hand, a number of authors suggest that there may indeed be notable effects of adult roles on interest. In primary analysis of the data used in this study, M. Kent Jennings and Richard G. Niemi find a slight increase in the gap between male and female levels of interest between 1965 and 1973.[15] This increase is accounted for by the fact that the men as a group increased in their level of interest in the eight years following high school while the women did not. Other observers of women's roles in politics, however, seem to suggest that the traditional roles of motherhood and homemaking, especially, may depress the amount of attention women are likely to pay to public affairs.[16]

Women's adult roles appear to have no significant effects on women's levels of political interest (Table 5:1).[17] The level of interest established by the time of high school graduation is clearly the best predictor of the later level; college education gives interest an additional boost.

Table 5:1
Determinants of Political Interest

Determinants	
1965 Interest	.33*
Education	.13*
Marriage	.06
Motherhood	−.03
Homemaking	.01
Privatization	−.04
R^2	.16
(N)	(664)

Note. Unless otherwise specified, data are drawn from 1973 wave of survey, entries are standardized regression coefficients throughout this chapter.
*$p < .05$.

Surely, one might argue, the mere degree of contact with the world outside the family must have an effect on employed women's political interest. Women who are bound by families, especially those who have no outside employment, are often claimed to be out of contact with the world of politics. Do homemakers have as much opportunity as do other women for socio-economic resources such as education to be converted into political interest? The answer is no, as shown in Table 5:2. If we compare the effects of education on the political interest of women with different marital and employment statuses, we find that education has significant effects only on those women who are both married and employed outside the home. Among the women who are both married and employed, 27 percent of the high school graduates said they followed politics "most of the time" compared with 58 percent of those with college education. As we can see, none of the female roles in and of themselves directly affect women's political interest. They can, however, affect the potential shaping influence of other socio-economic forces such as education. In this case, strong ties to both the private world of the family as well as the public world of the economy seem to open the way for receiving at least this benefit of education.

One further point about political interest is worth noting. A recurrent theme in discussion of women and politics is women's parochialism. When women are interested and involved in politics, many people suggest that women have unique "feminine" objects of interest.

Table 5:2
Determinants of Political Interest, by Marital and Employment Status

Determinants	Total Single	Married Employed	Married Homemaker	Total Married
1965 Interest	.31*	.34*	.33*	.34*
Education	.05	.23*	.04	.15*
Motherhood	−.12	.02	−.06	−.01
Homemaking	−	−	−	.01
Privatization	−.11	−.02	.01	−.02
R^2	.15	.21	.13	.16
(N)	(186)	(278)	(200)	(478)

Note. For further explanation see Table 5:1.
*$p < .05$.

These objects include those that are close to home and bear special relevance to women's domestic concerns such as local parks, schools, or health facilities.[18] Do women's domestic roles, as some seem to suggest, keep their interest from wandering to national and international politics? The women in the study were asked to report which level of government they paid most attention to when they followed current news on politics.[19] Table 5:3 shows the effects of women's roles on their attention to national and international as opposed to state and local politics. The more educated women were more likely to say they were interested in national and international politics. This was especially true for single women followed by married employed women, and least true for homemakers. Employment status itself has a direct effect on the object of married women's political interest; local politics is more likely to be the dominant concern of homemakers than is true of the employed.

Although the relationship between homemaking and women's interest in politics is fairly consistent with past suggestions, the relationship between motherhood and the object of political interest is not. Among homemakers mothers appear to be *more* interested in national and international as opposed to state and local politics than are women without children. Explanations for this finding can only be based on speculation here, but if we consider the reasons why young women might be homemakers today, it seems plausible to argue that childless homemakers are likely to be more parochial than homemakers with children. The labor force participation rates

Table 5:3

Determinants of Attention to National and International Politics,
by Marital and Employment Status

Determinants	Total	Single	Married Employed	Married Homemakers	Total Married
Education	.22*	.39*	.20*	.12	.17*
Marriage	.04	–	–	–	–
Motherhood	.07	–.05	.06	.15*	.10*
Homemaking	–.15	–	–	–	–.18*
Privatization	–.09*	–.10	–.04	–.07	–.08
R^2	.08	.17	.06	.07	.06
(N)	(629)	(175)	(265)	(188)	(454)

Note. For further explanation see Table 5:1.
*$p < .05$.

for young women is quite high; the presence of young children temporarily depresses that rate. Whereas we once asked why a young married woman would choose to seek employment, today the more interesting question may be why a young married woman without children would choose not to be employed. We might argue that the childless homemaker is likely to be bound more by traditional parochial values. We can further note that a college education promotes interest in national and international affairs, and relatively few of the childless homemakers have a college education.

Understanding Politics

One must have some basic knowledge or understanding of the political system in order to be integrated into it as a participant. Although expertise in political matters is not an essential basis for political participation, one must have at least a general idea of how government works as well as some specific pieces of information about politics and government in order to know how, when, or where one may participate. Past studies have found women lacking in this regard. Along with interest, a knowledge differential between the sexes is one of the earliest and most consistently found differences in childhood socialization studies.[20]

The norm of privatization should inhibit the development of political understanding. Among women who accept this norm, the centrality of their "private existence" should lead them to be somewhat less likely to seek, and especially to retain information about politics. Although these women may follow news of daily political events, this information should not be salient enough to be remembered. We may hypothesize that women who accept the traditional norm of privatization will have less understanding of politics than do those who reject it.

Insofar as gender roles place constraints on personal resources, we may also see some relationship between these roles and political understanding. The time and energy demands of motherhood, particularly when children are young, have been treated as factors that serve to remove women from the contact with politics necessary for information purposes. Naomi Lynn and Cornelia Flora, for example, demonstrate that communication networks of women with young children are relatively restricted and, in a sense, impermeable to political information.[21] We may therefore hypothesize that mothers will demonstrate less understanding of the political system than will women without children.

Homemaking as a sole occupation is identified as a cause of low levels of political knowledge among women. Sometimes this attribution is made only implicitly. The phrase, "women at home with children" refers to two different aspects of women's lives: (1) motherhood and (2) having no employment beside homemaking. This example serves as a case in point of the need to be clear about the specific aspects of women's roles that affect their political roles. Not all mothers of young children are solely homemakers. In this study 35 percent of the mothers without college education and 43 percent of the mothers with at least some college education were employed outside the home. There are reasons to suspect that homemaking itself inhibits the development of political understanding. Homemaking, especially for the young mother, is primarily a solitary occupation with little opportunity for political discussion with other adults. Until recently homemaking has not been viewed as a special interest occupation, one with specific political concerns that would draw a person into politics. Only with the growth of consumer advocacy movements and product boycotts have homemakers been viewed as an attentive political group.

Despite the intuitively pleasing nature of these observations about homemaking and its potential political effects, closer analysis reveals some flaws in hypothesizing a relationship between women's employment and political understanding. The housewife's home as her cloister is not as true an image as many people seem to believe. The homemaker's workplace includes not only her home but also the shopping center, post office, bank, and other areas of the community. Nor is the home impermeable to the full range of mass media through which political information is transmitted. Indeed, housewives spend more time exposed to mass media and engaged in reading than do employed women, and about the same as men.[22] Finally, although the homemaker's primary occupation is focused on the home, many are very involved in community activities, organizations, and volunteer work that bring them into closer contact with political issues and problems. Homemakers have slightly more free time to allow for these activities than do employed women.[23] Hypothesizing any direct relationship between women's employment status and levels of political knowledge would be unwarranted.

Traditional sociology of the family might lead one to hypothesize a relationship between marriage and political understanding. The functionalist model of family sociology posits one overriding form of role differentiation within a conjugal pair: the feminine expressive and the masculine instrumental. These norms are supposed to be reflected in the feminine responsibility for internal private concerns and masculine responsibility for external public and status-laden concerns. If "politics is man's business," the presence of a man in the house might accentuate the tendency for a woman to leave the responsibility of paying attention to politics to him. The authors of the *American Voter* conclude, for example, "The wife who votes but otherwise pays little attention to politics not only tends to leave the sifting of information up to her husband but abides by his ultimate decision about the direction of the vote as well. The information that she brings to bear on 'her' choice is indeed fragmentary, because it is second hand."[24] As in the case of occupational status, however, there are serious flaws in this hypothesis. The power of the notion of instrumental-expressive differentiation of men and women in marriage depends in large part on the assumption that in a "normal" family the husband devotes himself to the responsibilities of a job and the wife devotes herself to being his wife, the mother of his children, and the manager of his household.[25] Thus, even if this image could be accepted as normal, direct effects on political understanding would more likely come from motherhood or employment status than from marital status. In addition to the theoretical problems, many researchers seem to assert a division of political labor within marriage without providing evidence other than conventional wisdom. In one case where evidence was brought to bear on the question, Jennings and Niemi conclude that the "division of political labor" within the family is less differentiated than many researchers seem to assume.[26] The gender variables, with the exception of privatization, should have little clear, direct effect on political understanding.

Two variables are used here to tap political understanding. The first is political knowledge, scored to reflect the number of correct responses to six questions on specific political matters. Three concern awareness of the political system: the number of years in a senatorial term, the number of judges on the Supreme Court, and the name of the governor in the state in which the respondent resided. The other three concern political history and culture: Marshall Tito's nationality, the name of the country that interned Jews in concentration camps during World War II, and Franklin Delano Roosevelt's party affiliation. Political sophistication, devised by Philip Converse in his work on belief systems and ideology, is based on the respondents' understanding of the differences between the Republican and Democratic parties.[27] The responses are coded as follows: (1) Broad conceptual difference mentioned, (2) Narrow conceptual difference mentioned, (3) Some error in the response, (4) No difference between the parties perceived. This measure is controversial enough to merit discussion. Its use requires a set of assumptions. These are (1) that there are some fundamental differences between the parties;[28] (2) that these differences are not readily accessible without a relatively high level of understanding of the policies, orientations, and behavior of partisan elites; and (3) that expressions of differences may be categorized ordinally according to the degree of abstract conceptualization. Thus, the measure allows testing of the degree of sophistication in understanding at least one area of American politics: political parties.

The effects of women's roles on the two measures of political understanding are displayed in Table 5:4. The women's level of knowledge when they were high school seniors is by far the best predictor of their level of knowledge eight years later. In contrast, the 1965 conceptualization score is relatively less important in predicting the 1973 level of conceptualization. Conversely, college education is a relatively more important basis for developing conceptual sophistication than for obtaining or retaining basic political facts, as we might expect. Some basic political information is acquired during childhood; development of more sophisticated understanding occurs as a result of higher education or adult experience with the political system.[29]

Table 5:4
Determinants of Two Types of Political Understanding

Determinants	Knowledge	Sophistication
1965 Knowledge or Sophistication	.55*	.24*
Education	.18*	.32*
Marital	−.02	.03
Maternal	−.06	.01
Homemaking	.03	.03
Privatization	−.08*	−.16*
R^2	.46	.26
(N)	(554)	(554)

Note. For further explanation see Table 5:1.
*$p < .05$.

The hypotheses about the relationship between gender roles and political understanding receive moderate confirmation. As hypothesized, there is no apparent relationship between marital or employment status and either of the measures of understanding. Maternal status also has no significant direct effect on political understanding as measured here. In contrast, acceptance of the norm of privatization appears to inhibit the development of both political knowledge and an abstract conceptualization of politics, especially the latter. Abstract conceptualization of politics is often thought to be a technique of economy; those for whom politics is relatively salient need a system for categorizing or simplifying political information. These results suggest that traditional privatized women may have slightly less political information at their disposal, and are less in need of conceptual economies in this domain than are women who are more public oriented. Indeed, if we look at the bivariate relationship between conceptual sophistication and privatization, we find that among college-educated women 22 percent of the egalitarians and 56 percent of the traditionals could not correctly iden-

Table 5:5
Determinants of Two Types of Political Understanding,
by Marital and Employment Status

Determinants	Total Single	Married Employed	Married Homemaker	Total Married
Knowledge				
1965 Knowledge	.46*	.43*	.35*	.39*
Education	.11	.21*	.24*	.22*
Motherhood	−.04	−.10	−.04	−.10*
Homemaking	−	−	−	.03
Privatization	−.19*	−.03	−.10	−.07
R²	.38	.32	.28	.31
(N)	(167)	(226)	(161)	(387)
Sophistication				
1965 Sophistication	.15*	.29*	.27*	.28*
Education	.34*	.33*	.28*	.32*
Motherhood	−.14	.08	.01	.07
Homemaking	−	−	−	−.07
Privatization	−.13	−.11	−.21	−.16*
R²	.17	.29	.27	.29
(N)	(158)	(231)	(165)	(396)

Note. For further explanation see Table 5:1.
*p < .05.

tify any difference between the parties. Among the high school graduates 57 percent of the egalitarians and 82 percent of the traditionals demonstrated similar lack of awareness. If understanding the party system is at all a prerequisite for rational participation in American politics, traditionally oriented women are ill equipped.

Although marital and employment status have no direct effects on women's political understanding, do they have the same impact on the derived benefits of education as was the case for political interest? The answer, as Table 5:5 shows, is "yes and no." Let us first consider simple factual knowledge. The level of political knowledge the single and married employed women had in 1973 was more a function of earlier levels of knowledge than was true of homemakers. Regardless of employment, education has a greater effect on political knowledge among married women than is true for single women. Basic factual knowledge of this sort is more dependent upon precollege training than on college training; this is especially true for women who did not get married in the interim. The case is different for conceptual sophistication; here we see it is the single woman who benefits the most from college education. The effects of privatization also offer an interesting comparison. We have already seen that privatization depressed political knowledge, but not as much as it depresses sophistication. Now we see that these effects are role specific. Only single women's political knowledge is significantly depressed by privatization, only married women, and especially homemakers, are similarly affected in their levels of sophistication.

Political Efficacy

It is one thing to have a basic set of tools, such as knowledge, which one may use to cope with the political system; it is quite another to feel competent to participate. One of the psychological variables in political analysis that has received widespread attention in recent years is subjective political competence or a sense of political efficacy, the feeling that one is equipped to understand and deal with politics.

A sense of political efficacy is a particularly important aspect of a person's political personality. It is also a common theme in research on women and politics. As we have seen, contemporary analysts of democratic theory regard political efficacy as crucial for democratic participation and citizenship. Pateman's[30] discussion of self-confidence and control as part of efficacy demonstrates the importance of the concept for women: these are exactly the personality characteristics which have been inhibited in women.[31] Numerous studies show that women tend to devalue or underestimate their abilities in tasks that are labeled as "belonging" to the other sex.[32] Married women exhibit more symptoms of mental health problems, especially depression, than do men. Women who have lived lives that conform most closely to traditional conceptions of women's roles, i.e., those who are homemakers and invest the greatest proportion of their psychic and physical energy in their families, are the most likely to be faced with severe middle-aged depression and crises in self-confidence.[33] Many people have argued that the surest evidence for the widespread oppression of women is the depressed sense of an autonomous, competent self exhibited by women.[34]

Past research has shown women less likely than men to have a strong subjective sense of civic competence. Analysis of sex differences in political efficacy led the authors of *The American Voter* to conclude that "men are more likely than women to feel that they can cope with the complexities of politics and to believe that their participation carries some weight in the political process."[35] This idea has become part of the conventional wisdom on women and politics. Curiously, analysis of national election data over the last twenty years suggests that generalized statements about sex differences in efficacy need more qualification than is often offered. In single item analysis of the efficacy questions in Michigan election studies from 1952 to 1972, John Soule and Wilma McGrath find sex differences of at least ten percentage points on only one item, but this difference appears at each time point sampled.[36] This question, which asks respondents to agree or disagree with the statement, "Sometimes politics and government seem so complicated that a person like me can't really understand what's going on," captures very precisely traditional notions of women's relationship to politics: politics is man's business, women are simply not capable of understanding it.

Most empirical treatments of political efficacy use a measure comprised of all five of the questions Soule and McGrath analyzed. This scale has recently been the subject of considerable criticism.[37] One of these criticisms is of particular relevance here. The "standard" efficacy scale includes questions that relate to one's own sense of internal competence (e.g., being able to understand politics) as well as questions that have more to do with competence based on external constraints (e.g., public officials don't care what I think). As a result, many researchers now use two different measures of political efficacy. One, the "external" sense of efficacy, taps the degree to which one feels that *others* make it possible to exert influence in politics. The other, more to the point of this discussion, measures an "internal" sense of political efficacy, the degree to which one feels he or she has the personal, especially psychological, resources to exert influence. Interestingly, only one of the questions appears to refer to internal efficacy unambiguously. This item, which concerns the ability to understand politics, is the one on which sex differences have been found consistently. For this reason, our analysis focuses on this question.

Prior research suggests that specific adult roles help shape political efficacy. In original analysis of these data M. Kent Jennings and Richard Niemi show that internal efficacy dropped more among women from 1965 to 1973 than it did among men, thus accentuating the difference between the sexes. They attribute the change to the life-cycle effects of young adulthood.[38] Naomi Lynn and Cornelia Flora found mothers less efficacious than were childless women.[39] Angus Campbell and his colleagues appear to attribute low levels of efficacy in women to their conjugal roles, arguing that the division of labor in the family leaves women with a feeling that politics is not their business.[40] Kristi Andersen shows that homemakers feel less competent to deal with politics than do employed women.[41] Further, if a depression of efficacy is associated with a sense of distance or lack of connection (and therefore a lack of understanding), privatization should also inhibit the development of a strong sense of political self.

If we examine the effects of women's roles on political efficacy we find, as Lynn and Flora suggested, that motherhood inhibits the development of efficacy, as does privatization (Table 5:6). Those women who feel more bound to the private world of the family feel less competent to deal with politics than do other women. Although these relationships are small, it is noteworthy that motherhood and privatization serve at least as well as predictors of efficacy as does education, which is usually thought to be an important basis for the development of subjective competence.

Table 5:6
Determinants of Political Efficacy

Determinants	
1965 Political Efficacy	.17*
Education	.09*
Marriage	.00
Motherhood	−.08*
Homemaking	−.06
Privatization	−.09*
R^2	.08
(N)	(663)

Note. For further explanation see Table 5:1.
*p < .05.

Psychological studies show a tendency for women to underestimate themselves, to underjudge their own competence especially in "male" tasks and areas of expertise. If this is true, in politics we should find evidence in the relationship of subjective measures of political competence to "objective" measures of political competence. To what degree do women's feelings about how much they understand politics depend upon resources such as education, information, and analytical sophistication? If women's roles inhibit the development of subjective competence as distinct from objective competence, we should find that these resources have less bearing on political efficacy among women involved in traditional roles than among women who are not. The test of this hypothesis is very straightforward; we can examine the degree to which the political efficacy of women in different roles is predicted by their levels of knowledge, conceptual sophistication, and education.

Women's roles do make a difference in the degree to which women's feelings of competence are linked to more objective indicators of competence (Table 5:7). Although the total amount of variance explained is not impressive in any case, motherhood and homemaking appear to be particular inhibitors of the development of political efficacy. Looking at the specific predictors, basic factual knowledge is a more clear and stable basis for a sense of competence among single, childless, employed, and "public-oriented" women than it is among married or childless women, homemakers, and those who accept the ideology of privatization. Interestingly, conceptual sophistication, a "harder" test of competence than factual knowledge, is a strong basis for a sense of competence only among the privatized women. Traditional women's roles inhibit the development of one of the most important psychological resources for participatory citizenship: a sense of self-confidence. The moral of the story is, if a woman claims that her pretty little head can't cope with the difficult problems of politics, it is not necessary to believe her. For women in traditional roles, competence is not translated into feelings of competence as much as it is for other women.

Political Trust

In recent years feminists have been suggesting that women have been taught to understand their problem in precisely the wrong way.

Table 5:7

Effects of Education and Political Understanding on Political Efficacy, by Roles and Privatization

Determinants	Marital		Maternal		Employment		Privatization	
	Single	Married	No Children	Children	Employed	Homemaker	Low	High
Knowledge	.20*	.11*	.17*	.04	.17*	.17	.17*	.01
Sophistication	.06	.10	.07	.09	.09	.08	-.06	.27*
Education	.05	.10	.08	.09	.08	.03	.11	-.14
R^2	.07	.05	.07	.01	.07	.01	.05	.07
(N)	(163)	(384)	(278)	(269)	(382)	(165)	(265)	(75)

Note. For further explanation see Table 5:1.
*p < .05.

The argument maintains that whereas women have had a relatively low sense of self-worth and tend to undervalue their own competence, they have been far too dependent upon and trustful of other authorities, especially their husbands. A "feminist consciousness" as suggested in Chapter 4, involves an awareness of the limitations placed on women by political and economic institutions. In a political context, if women are unduly trustful in the good will of authorities, there would be little reason for agitation for change.

Research on women suggests that women are more trustful in and deferent to authority, including political authority, than are men.[42] Even women's verbal and nonverbal styles of communication are imbued with indications of deference.[43] Beside the training to dependence women receive, there are reasons to believe that women's adult roles help foster trust. One of women's most basic roles is to entrust her well-being to the man she marries. Traditionally a wife is dependent upon her husband, and husbands tend to serve as mediators between the wife and the outside world. One might argue that those who blithely leave power over themselves to others — as women do in the home, the marketplace, and the polity — must have greater trust in the beneficence of other's authority than do those who would prefer to reserve power over themselves *for* themselves.

Thus, Harriet Holter's review of research on women and authority leads her to suggest that as women are faced with a relatively benign form of authority, and perhaps a need to justify relinquishing many forms of self-determination, women will be more accepting of and deferent to authority.[44] In addition, Thomas Volgy and Sandra Volgy demonstrate that women who reject traditional ideas of women in the home are less trusting in political authority than are women who accept the norm of privatization.[45] The view proposed here is similar to Fred Greenstein's discussion of generalization of benevolent patriarchal authority.[46]

This study includes five questions relating to political trust.[47] Only two trust items bear any relationship to women's roles, including the acceptance and rejection of the norm of privatization, and on one, the relationship holds only among those with some college education. Among women who had some college education, 61 percent of the egalitarians and 41 percent of those who believe women's place is in the home thought that the government is "run by a few big interests." The privatized women had more faith that the government is "run for the benefit of all"; they are more likely to see a benevolent, all-caring authority.

The trust question that merits attention is one which asks how often the women felt they could trust government officials. This is the only question that concerns trust in the *people* in power per se, which approximates the type of trust referred to by prior research on women. As we suggested, there is a direct relationship between marital status and trust in political authorities (Table 5:8). Among the college-educated women, 31 percent of the wives and 53 percent of the single women said they trust government officials "only some of the time." This attitude about government officials is also held by 21 percent of the wives and 38 percent of the single women who did not go to college. The substantive significance of this relationship is underscored by the observation that it is at least as strong as the relationship between the earlier and later levels of trust. Moreover, marriage seems to promote trust at least as much as higher education appears to deflate it.

Table 5:8
Determinants of Political Trust

Determinants	
1965 Political Trust	.14*
Education	-.11*
Marriage	.17*
Motherhood	.00
Homemaking	.01
Privatization	.07
R^2	.07
(N)	(659)

Note. For further explanation see Table 5:1.
*$p < .05$.

One point that must be remembered is that political trust in general dropped considerably in the late 1960s and early 1970s. Thus it might be more accurate to say that during that period marriage may have helped buffer women against as great a loss in faith as they might otherwise have experienced rather than arguing that marriage developed trust in women. More evidence is provided by

Jennings's and Niemi's original analysis of their data. Both the men and women in the study became less trusting in government from 1965 to 1973, although this was particularly true among men. As a result, male-female differences were greater among the young adults than they were among the high school seniors. Jennings and Niemi offer two tentative explanations. One is that the "greater interest, knowledge, and participation on the part of young males helped them shed more quickly any remaining youthful idealism." They also suggest that males may have been more responsive to the external stimuli of the times.[48] Although our discussion does not focus on sex differences, the point is similar to Jennings and Niemi's second suggestion. The present argument is that marriage may have served as a block to some of the external stimuli of the times. If this is true, there should be more continuity in trust among the married women between 1965 and 1973 than among those who were single.

Further analysis shows that this is the case (Table 5:9). There is no connection between 1965 and 1973 levels of trust among single women, almost as if they were more exposed to the turbulent late 1960s and the dawning of the Watergate revelations. Among the married women only those who are employed appear affected by higher education, although employment itself has no direct effect on trust. Once again it appears that employment is an important agent for married women in the sense that it creates an opportunity for women to be shaped by — or to use — their education.

Table 5:9
Determinants of Political Trust, by Marital and Employment Status

Determinants	Single	Married Employed	Married Homemaker	Total Married
1965 Political Trust	.04	.23*	.16*	.19*
Education	−.12	−.16*	−.04	−.10*
Motherhood	−.01	.03	−.03	.01
Homemaking	—	—	—	.0ᶜ
Privatization	.09	.03	.09	.ᶜ
R²	.03	.07	.03	
(N)	(185)	(277)	(197)	

Note. For further explanation see Table 5:1.
*p < .05.

Political Involvement and Citizenship

Verba, Nie, and Kim's work shows that psychological orientations toward politics and participation are important resources for participation.[49] The different approaches to theories of democratic participation suggest that we should also understand these orientations as, in part, demonstrations of the significance of politics and participation in politics. It is quite possible, especially in a political culture in which participation is in part seen as a duty or a source of support, for participation to be merely a sign of acquiescence as opposed to an attempt to use the government as a means to achieve desired ends.

The analysis presented here shows that women's adult roles shape the type of orientations women may bring to bear on political participation. A traditional combination of women's roles depressed women's understanding of politics and political efficacy and serves as a support for political trust. It also promotes the self-devaluation so common among women. Together these orientations form a clear picture of the acquiescent member of a political community.

There are numerous ways of understanding one's connection to the political system; the active, rational citizen is only one of them. Thus far this characterization does not fit the traditionally oriented woman. More evidence is provided by the women's responses to a question which asked them to define the attributes of a good citizen.[50] If traditional privatized women have different civic orientations from other women, the differences should be revealed here.

Table 5:10 shows the relationship between privatization and definitions of citizenship. The definitions are collapsed into three categories. The first includes women who mention *political support*; to them a good citizen is one who serves or respects the country, obeys laws, pays taxes, or is loyal to or uncritical of the government. These are political responses, but they express a passive orientation, and, as Jennings and Niemi suggest, resemble Almond and Verba's "subject" orientation toward politics.[51]

The second category includes those who mentioned more *active orientations* toward politics. This category is further subdivided into those reponses that mentioned only voting, which for many people may more reasonably be placed in the "support" category, and any other activism responses. These are Almond and Verba's "citizens," those who most certainly feel loyalty and respect are important civic

Table 5:10
Definitions of Attributes of a "Good Citizen,"
by Level of Privatization

Citizenship Attributes	Privatization		
	Low (%)	Medium (%)	High (%)
Political			
Support	22	23	39
Activism	68	61	53
(Vote)	(12)	(16)	(13)
(Other)	(56)	(46)	(41)
Nonpolitical	11	16	8
Total	101	100	100
(N)	(273)	(214)	(79)

Note. Entries represent the proportion within each category of privatization mentioning the various definitions. "Activism" is further broken down into those who mentioned only *voting* and those who mentioned *other* forms of political activism.

virtues, but who feel that the distinguishing characteristic of a good citizen is some form of political activism.

The last category contains responses that are *not explicitly political.* These include personal virtues such as religious and ethical values, interpersonal and personal characteristics, and independence and ambition. Although the responses may be seen as Almond and Verba's "parochials" or "pre-politicals," the women's movements' emphasis on the political attributes of personal or "non-political" acts makes this analogy difficult to maintain completely in this analysis.

This analysis lends added support to the observation that women's gender roles help create different citizenship roles. Privatized women comprise the group most likely to see citizenship as dependent upon support; they are least likely to view citizenship as a matter of activism and particularly, activism that goes beyond casting ballots from time to time.

Proof of the integration of women into a political community depends on much more than the relative likelihood that men and women participate in basic acts of citizenship. We would also have to know that the roles women are expected to play in their private lives do not help maintain a tendency toward subject status and orientations. Unfortunately this is not the case. Adult roles are not the major determinants of political orientations; a large portion of the variance is explained by childhood experiences, as indicated by the effects of the 1965 orientations, and, as is common in survey research, a more substantial portion of the variance is left unexplained. But a synthesis of the findings presented here suggests the inhibiting features of womens' roles. It is clear that the growing trend toward increased education for women is critical to their political development. As education becomes less gender defined, so will political orientations. Marriage, homemaking, and motherhood, and the norm of privatization also help structure political orientations and resources, although each in different ways.

As long as gender roles continue to create divisions of labor into "male" and "female" tasks, they will continue to depress women's feelings or competence in male domains, including politics, regardless of their actual level of expertise. If wives, like children, are buffered from the outside world through a division of labor that makes it the husband's job to deal with outside authorities, women may have an inflated sense of trust in those authorities — things usually "work out" with very little effort on their part. Women who continue to believe that women's place is in the home may well be interested in politics, but what will their style of interaction with politics be? A strong possibility is that they may continue to be good "helpmeets" to the government (being loyal, paying their taxes), just as they may be good "helpmeets" to their husbands. Women's roles no longer exclude them from politics at the mass level, but the remains of traditional women's roles still inhibit the development of the woman citizen.

NOTES

1. Gabriel Almond and Sidney Verba, *The Civic Culture* (Boston: Little, Brown, 1965), p. 120.
2. See also Carole Pateman, *Participation and Democratic Theory* (New York: Cambridge University Press, 1970), p. 110.
3. Perhaps the foremost representative is Robert A. Dahl, *A Preface to Democratic Theory* (Chicago: University of Chicago Press, 1956). See Pateman's excellent review and critique of this approach in *Participation and Democratic Theory*. For an analysis of women and political

representation see Virginia Sapiro, "When Are Interests Interesting? The Problem of Political Representation of Women," *American Political Science Review* 75 (Sept., 1981), 701-16.

4. The most well known representatives of this notion of limitations to democratic participation are Seymour Martin Lipset, *Political Man* (New York: Doubleday, 1960) and Samuel P. Huntington, *Political Order in Changing Societies* (New Haven: Yale University Press, 1968).

5. Although not usually considered as part of the literature on democratic theory, the best work on this approach is Murray Edelman, *The Symbolic Uses of Politics* (Urbana: University of Illinois Press, 1964).

6. Pateman, *Participation and Democratic Theory*, pp. 45-46.

7. Sidney Verba, Norman H. Nie, and Jae-on Kim, *Participation and Political Equality: A Seven Nation Comparison* (Cambridge: Cambridge University Press, 1978).

8. *Ibid.*, pp. 8-9.

9. Sidney Verba, Norman Nie, Jae-on Kim, and Goldie Shabad, "Men and Women: Sex-Related Differences in Political Activity," in Verba, Nie, and Kim, *Participation and Political Equality*, pp. 235-37.

10. Verba, Nie, Kim, and Shabad, "Men and Women," p. 262.

11. Pateman, *Participation and Democratic Theory*, especially Chapter III; Almond and Verba, *The Civic Culture*.

12. Judy Bertelsen, "Political Interest, Influence, and Efficacy: Differences between the Sexes and among Marital Status Groups," *American Politics Quarterly* 2 (Oct., 1974), 412-26; Fred I. Greenstein, *Children and Politics* (New Haven: Yale University Press, 1969); Margaret L. Inglehart, "Political Interest in West European Women: An Historical and Empirical Comparative Analysis," paper delivered at the Annual Meeting of the Midwest Political Science Association, Chicago, 1979; Anthony Orum, Roberta Cohen, Sherri Grasmuck, and Amy Orum, "Sex, Socialization, and Politics," *American Sociological Review* 39 (Apr., 1974), 197-209; Verba, Nie, Kim, and Shabad, "Men and Women."

13. Greenstein, *Children and Politics*, p. 114.

14. *Ibid.*, p. 116.

15. M. Kent Jennings and Richard G. Niemi, *Generations and Politics: Young Adults and Their Parents* (Princeton: Princeton University Press, 1981).

16. For example, Robert Lane, *Political Life* (New York: Free Press, 1959).

17. "Political Interest" is drawn from responses to the question, "Some people seem to think about what's going on in government and public affairs most of the time, whether there's an election going on or not. Others aren't that interested. Would you say you follow what's going on in government and public affairs most of the time, some of the time, only now and then, or hardly at all?"

18. Lane, *Political Life.* For empirical evidence, see M. Kent Jennings, "Another Look at the Life Cycle and Political Participation," *American Journal of Political Science* 23 (Nov., 1979), 755-71.

19. After being asked how often they follow politics the respondents were asked, "Which one do you follow most closely — international affairs, national affairs, state affairs, or local affairs?"

20. Robert Dowse and John Hughes, "Girls, Boys, and Politics," *British Journal of Sociology* 22 (Mar., 1971), 53-67; Greenstein, *Children and Politics;* Veronica Stolte Heiskanen, "Sex Roles, Social Class, and Political Consciousness," *Acta Sociologica* 14 (1971), 83-95; Herbert Hyman, *Political Socialization* (Glencoe: Free Press, 1959); M. Kent Jennings and Richard G. Niemi, *The Political Character of Adolescence* (Princeton: Princeton University Press, 1974); Orum et al., "Sex, Socialization, and Politics."

21. Cornelia B. Flora and Naomi B. Lynn, "Women and Political Socialization: Considerations of the Impact of Motherhood," in Jane Jaquette, ed., *Women in Politics* (New York: Wiley, 1974), pp. 37-53; Naomi B. Lynn and Cornelia B. Flora, "Motherhood and Political Participation: The Changing Sense of Self," *Journal of Political and Military Sociology* 1 (Spring, 1973), 91-103.

22. John Robinson, Philip Converse, and Alexander Szalai, "Everyday Life in Twelve Countries," in Alexander Szalai, ed., *The Use of Time* (The Hague: Mouton Publishers, 1972), pp. 137-38.

23. This is not to say that homemakers engage in these activities more than men do. The point is only that the opportunity is available. Robinson, Converse, and Szalai, "Everyday Life in Twelve Countries."

24. Angus Campbell, Philip Converse, Warren Miller, and Donald Stokes, *The American Voter* (New York: Wiley, 1964), pp. 260-61.

25. Talcott Parsons, *The Social System* (New York: Macmillan, 1951), pp. 224-25; Parsons et al., *Family, Socialization, and Interaction Process* (Glencoe: Free Press, 1954), pp. 94-95.

26. M. Kent Jennings and Richard G. Niemi, "The Division of Labor between Mothers and Fathers," *American Political Science Review* 65 (Mar., 1971), 69-82.

27. Philip E. Converse, "The Nature of Belief Systems in Mass Publics," in David Apter, ed., *Ideology and Discontent* (Glencoe: Free Press, 1964), pp. 206-62. Women have been found to score relatively low on this and similar measures compared with men; see M. Kent Jennings and Barbara E. Farah, "Ideology, Gender, and Political Action: A Cross-National Survey," *British Journal of Political Science* 10 (Apr., 1980), 219-40.

28. Despite popular cynicism about political parties, empirical elite studies show that partisan elites — that is, the people who set the party agenda, develop party proposals, and have power over political careers, differ in ideology and role interpretation along party lines. The validity of this measure depends on party differences, not party responsiveness.

29. See also M. Kent Jennings and Richard G. Niemi, "Continuity and Change in Political Orientations: A Longitudinal Study of Two Generations," *American Political Science Review* 69 (Dec., 1975), 1316-35.

30. Pateman, *Participation and Democratic Theory.*

31. For reviews of these studies, see Kay Deaux, *The Behavior of Women and Men* (Monterey, Calif.: Wadsworth Publishing, 1976) and Irene Frieze et al., eds., *Women and Sex Roles: A Social Psychological Perspective* (New York: W.W. Norton, 1978).

32. Deaux, *The Behavior of Women and Men,* Chapters 3 and 4.

33. On studies of mental health, see Jeanne Maracek, "Psychological Disorders in Women: Indices of Role Strain," in Frieze et al., *Women and Sex Roles,* pp. 255-76.

34. Among these see Virginia Sapiro, "Sex and Games: On Oppression and Rationality," *British Journal of Political Science* 9 (Oct., 1979), 385-408.

35. Campbell, Converse, Miller, and Stokes, *The American Voter,* p. 259.

36. John W. Soule and Wilma E. McGrath, "A Comparative Study of Male-Female Political Attitudes at Citizen and Elite Levels," in Marianne Githens and Jewel Prestage, eds., *A Portrait of Marginality: The Political Behavior of the American Woman* (New York: Longman, 1977), p. 183.

37. For example, J. Miller McPherson, Susan Welch, and Cal Clark, "The Stability and Reliability of Political Efficacy: Using Path Analysis to Test Alternative Models," *American Political Science Review* 71 (June, 1977), 509-21.

38. Jennings and Niemi, *Generations and Politics.*

39. Lynn and Flora, "Motherhood and Political Participation."

40. Campbell, Converse, Miller, and Stokes, *The American Voter,* p. 260.

41. Kristi Andersen, "Working Women and Political Participation, 1952-1972," *American Journal of Political Science* 19 (May, 1975), 444.

42. For a discussion of these studies, see especially, Harriet Holter, *Sex Roles and Social Structure* (Oslo: Universitetsforlaget, 1971).

43. Nancy Henley, *Body Politics* (Englewood Cliffs: Prentice-Hall, 1977); Nancy Henley and Barrie Thorne, eds., *Language and Sex* (Rowley: Newbury House, 1975); Mary Ritchie Kay, *Male/Female Language* (Metuchen: Scarecrow Press, 1975). See also Chapter 6, this volume.

44. Holter, *Sex Roles and Social Structure.*

45. Thomas Volgy and Sandra Volgy, "Women and Politics: Political Correlates of Sex-Role Acceptance," *Social Science Quarterly* 55 (Mar., 1975), 967-74.

46. Greenstein, *Children and Politics.* One might argue with the direction of causality suggested here. However, because the vast majority of women marry at least once it is unlikely that they make their decisions about whether or not to marry on the basis of generalized trust in authority. As Helena Lopata points out in *Occupation: Housewife*

(New York: Oxford, 1971), one of the most difficult features of the marital adjustment period is adapting to dependence. This analogy is, of course, limited to the cases in which the patriarchal authority is indeed benevolent or perceived that way.

47. The trust questions are:
    (1) ". . . over the years, how much attention do you feel the government pays to what the people think when it decides what to do, a good deal, some, or not much?"
    (2) "Do you think that quite a few of the people running the government are dishonest, not very many are, or do you think hardly any of them are dishonest?"
    (3) "Do you think that people in the government waste a lot of the money we pay in taxes, waste some of it, or don't waste very much of it?"
    (4) "How much of the time do you think you can trust the government in Washington to do what is right — just about always, most of the time or only some of the time?"
    (5) "Do you think that almost all of the people running the government are smart people who usually know what they are doing, or do you think that quite a few of them don't seem to know what they are doing?"
    (6) "Would you say the government is pretty much run by a few big interests looking out for themselves or that it is run for the benefit of all the people?"

48. Jennings and Niemi, *Generations and Politics.*

49. Verba, Nie, and Kim, *Participation and Political Equality.*

50. "People have different ideas about what being a good citizen means. We're interested in what you think. Tell me how you would describe a good citizen in this country — that is, what things about a person are most important in showing that one is a good citizen."

51. Jennings and Niemi, *The Political Character of Adolescence,* pp. 120-21.

CHAPTER 6

Political Communication, Participation, and Influence

The central focus of much of the research on women and politics is political participation. The fight for the opportunity to vote has been the most publicized battle in the long history of feminism. As Chapter 2 pointed out, feminists had great, largely unfulfilled expectations about the impact of women's use of that opportunity on government and politics.

Today few people would suggest that voting and other conventional mass-level political activities are improper for women. In recent years sex differences in electoral and other forms of participation have diminished considerably. Susan Hansen and her colleagues find, "As of 1972, rates of voting, campaign activism, and political letter writing among college educated or working women were equal to or greater than those of men of similar SES levels."[1] This observation, along with the results of other research on women and politics, suggests that women's private roles continue to shape the levels and types of participation in which women are engaged. As Chapter 5 shows, roles affect the psychological orientations women bring to bear on political activity. Other studies, which will be discussed below, suggest that motherhood, employment, and gender role orientations have direct effects on political participation.

Most analyses of women's political participation focus exclusively on electoral activities. If one is interested in the degree to which women are full participating members of the political system, this type of analysis presents a number of problems. First, voting is a dubious test of citizenship. As we have seen, voting is not neces-sarily indicative of anything other than paying ritual fealty to the political system of which one is a member. Indeed, one of the unsolved puzzles occupying the time of many political scientists is the determination of whether voting is even a rational act.[2] We are not yet certain it is.

A second problem with limiting analyses of participation to elec-toral activities is that even if we look at campaign activities other than voting, we are talking about periodic participation in a local, state, or, more likely, national event. Politics and government are constants. In order to measure the degree of integration of any group into politics we would need to know more about the types of par-ticipation that can go on in between our regularly scheduled elections.

A third problem is that many of the political activities in which women have been involved the longest and most influentially are not electoral activities. As Chapter 2 discussed, women were active in political organizations, especially at the local level, long before they were allowed to vote. Women, especially feminists, have often used nonconventional political activities such as marches and demonstrations in order to press their demands on government. These activities cannot be judged less important or less political than electoral participation. Politics involves strategies of influence; there are many political situations in which electoral activities are simply inappropriate, ineffectual, or — for women — unavailable strategies for desired goals.

Our interest in women's political participation is one of discover-ing the degree to which women are willing and able to use political organizations and processes to let their political preferences be heard and, ultimately, to influence others. The point here is not so much to see whether women are "good citizens" who are actively involved in politics, but rather to find out whether women's private roles affect the types of political strategies women may use in pursuit of desired ends. The question is, really, to find out whether women have the means to be *effective* citizens. With this in mind we will discuss three types of political activity: political communication intended to influence others, electoral participation, and community participation.

Political Communication and Influence

Research on women and communication suggests that women's ability to participate in politics may be restricted at the most basic level, in their ability to make their desires known and influence others. Public stereotypes and research results differ considerably in the image of women and communication they present. Cartoons and stand-up comedians would have us believe that one of the most fatal diseases known to man is women's speech. Research findings tell us something quite different.

Male and female language styles and skills begin to diverge at a very young age. Girls develop verbal skills at a younger age, and women tend to speak more correctly than men do.[3] Women's skill at grammar, however, says little about the effectiveness of their communication. Most studies of male and female language reveal women as considerably less influential than are men. In settings including both women and men, women talk less than men do. The reason is not solely that women are shyer and quieter; rather, the problem is that men don't let them speak and, moreover, don't let them speak effectively. Men interrupt women more than they interrupt each other and more than women interrupt men. Studies of conversations show that men "kill" women's conversations by ignoring topics women raise or by changing the subject. Partly as a result of male conversational techniques, women and men take very different roles in mixed group discussions. Men initiate topics, make statements, and engage in other instrumental verbal acts. Women respond and react, ask questions, and engage in more expressive verbal acts.[4]

Research by Edward Megargee shows the importance of studying male-female interaction as a basis for understanding processes of influence.[5] In his study, Megargee administered tests for psychological dominance in both women and men. He then paired his subjects in single-sex and mixed-sex dyads. Each pair consisted of one person who was high on dominance and one who was not. Each pair was asked to decide which person would be the leader and which would be the follower within the pair for a later task. In the same-sex pairs, regardless of whether they were male or female, the person who was high on dominance was picked as the leader in 70 percent of the cases. In the mixed-sex pairs in which the man was high on dominance and the woman was not, the man was chosen as the leader in 90 percent of the cases. In the mixed-sex pairs in which the woman was high on dominance and the man was not, the woman was chosen as the leader in 20 percent of the cases. We do not have detailed information on the dynamics of those discussion sessions, but a wealth of experimental game research shows consistently that gender roles are important determinants of bargaining and decision-making processes in mixed groups.[6] Women are particularly likely to yield to men's judgments in areas of traditional male expertise — including politics.[7]

When men allow women the chance to communicate, their styles are quite different, and these differences are reinforced by social sanctions and incentives. A number of studies of communication and influence use Bertram Raven's categorization of six power bases, including reward and coercion, referent power (identification), expert power, legitimate power, and informational power. In addition, influence can be attempted through direct or indirect means, through personal or concrete resources, or on the basis of competence or helplessness.[8] Women are particularly likely to use referent power, and have less opportunity to use legitimate or expert power because of institutional discrimination. In addition, the types of power women use are modified by the more feminine styles of indirectness, personal resources, and appeals of helplessness.[9] An example of the significance of these differences is that women are seen in more negative terms when they transmit information directly rather than indirectly, while the reverse is true for men. The power styles that are acceptable for women are manipulative and "sneaky," which reinforces stereotypes of women.[10]

Even the language men and women use differs in form and style.[11] Women's language shows more uncertainty — particularly about themselves — and deference than does men's. They use more personalisms ("In my opinion . . . ," "I think . . .") and, especially, more personalisms that show self-doubt ("I may be crazy, but . . . ," "I may be wrong, but . . . ," "It's only my opinion, but . . ."). Women's use of intonation turns statements into questions. Common examples are found in everyday existence. One of the most common is a variant of the following. A woman is cooking dinner, and is waiting for the rice to be finished. Anyone who has ever cooked rice knows that once rice begins to cook, it must be carefully timed or else it may develop the consistency of library paste. The man asks, "When will dinner be ready?" The woman answers, "In five minutes?" Women also add tag questions that have a similar effect ("Dinner will be ready in five minutes, ok?"). The common types of tag questions women use show self-doubt or ask permission. Although these differences in language are, by and large, nonconscious, they limit women's ability to communicate and to influence. One study of jury behavior, for example, shows that women's language — regardless of whether it is delivered by a man or a woman — is less credible and less influential than men's. Research on nonverbal communication shows similar results. Women's posture, their mannerisms, and their use of space differs from men's in that it is less assertive, shows less indication of self-confidence and more deference.[12]

Women's language and communication styles and the styles men use against them may provide an important key to women's styles of political influence as well as the likelihood that they are successful. Recent analyses of the strategies employed by women's groups concerned with feminist issues reveal the importance of verbal and nonverbal communication styles. Feminists quickly became aware of the problems they had with their image when attempting to lobby on behalf of proposals such as the Equal Rights Amendment. Proponents are constantly warned to be "ladylike." Janet K. Boles reports one lobbyist explaining the usual strategy: "You end up being as ladylike as you can, as sweet, as charming. You get your hair fixed on the days you speak for the ERA and you wear your ERA dress wardrobe."[13] Stereotypes of female incompetence, especially at communication, are quite strong. Boles quoted another supporter voicing a problem many feminists have encountered: "It's a 'catch-22.' If you argue in an emotional way, they say you're 'only a woman.' If you debate logically and effectively, they say you're too mannish. After some of our wives and mothers testified for the amendment, the gossip around the State House the next day was that they were fakes. They couldn't have been *real* mothers because they spoke too well."[14]

Another study shows how "feminine tactics" can work if they are used in a manner that appears consistent with the women involved. In her study of lobbying efforts by the National Organization of Women and right-wing groups over schoolbook adoption in Texas,

Bonnie Cook-Freeman demonstrates the effectiveness of the lobbying techniques of self-consciously "female" females. She writes that
"right wing women make a point of developing friendly, credible
relationships with these members of the Board, particularly the conservative men who are most likely to cater to their concerns."[15]

> In fact, the right-wing consciously develops particular strate-
> gies for informal contact during the monthly meetings in Austin.
> Several women always travel to Austin, arranging to stay in
> the same hotel where Board members reside. The women also
> have their meals where the Board members eat. In this way,
> they maximize opportunities to talk with Board members. Some
> of these women are even willing to use conversation pieces to
> draw attention to themselves in order to initiate conversation.
> For example, one woman wears a variety of exotic hats to
> attract attention. She also frequently discusses sex. The other
> women enter dining halls first where the Board members are
> already seated and begin conversations with the Board mem-
> bers about what hat this woman may be wearing on that par-
> ticular day. This is their "in" to continue social and political
> exchange with members of the Board.[16]

Cook-Freeman's analysis of the right-wing strategies reads like a
page from a textbook on female use of manipulative power styles.

We have good reason to believe that women's roles may affect
the types of political influence strategies in which women become
engaged. The "feminine" power styles reflect women's self-concept;
that is, they are the strategies of people who are either lacking in
self-esteem or who must use deference to obtain their goals. Different acts of political influence require different skills, styles, and
resources. Although as the examples cited above show that one
strategy, lobbying, may be adapted to different role requirements,
some strategies may be more flexible or more congruent with traditional interpretations of feminine interaction than are others. We
should expect women who accept the ideology of privatization to
differ in their influence strategies from those who do not. Moreover, women's roles affect women's experience with different forms
of communication and influence as well the networks of communication available to them. Naomi Lynn and Cornelia Flora, for
example, show that the severely limited communication networks
of homemakers with young children may help remove women from

the possibility of becoming involved in discussions of politics, much less becoming involved in political influence.[17]

Unfortunately the data employed in this study do not permit analysis of the effectiveness of women's communication and influence attempts, but they do provide a basis for exploring the effects of women's roles on their ability or willingness to become involved in different types of strategies of influence. Four will be analyzed here: talking to people in an attempt to influence their ideas about politics, contacting public officials, writing letters to editors of public periodicals, and participating in protests or demonstrations.

We have already discussed the problems involved in women's attempts to talk and to convince. Throughout women's history, the more public women's communication was, the more it involved as its target strangers, and especially men, the more this communication was a subject of discussion, argument, horror, and derision. Early in American history women began to find public communication, especially writing in public periodicals, a means to express their will. In the beginning, many did so only reluctantly. "Belinda" wrote in *The New Jersey Gazette* in 1778, for example, "I do not remember whether your *Gazette* has hitherto given us the production of any woman correspondent — Indeed nothing but the most pressing call of my country could have induced me to appear in print. But rather than suffer your sex to be caught by the bait of that arch foe of American Liberty, Lord North, I think ours ought, to a woman, to draw their pens, and enter our solemn protest against it."[18] Despite objections on the part of men and many women, women became increasingly involved in making their views known through this means. As for direct contacts with public officials, until women gained the right to vote there was little else a woman could do if she felt moved to influence an official. One of the important strategies of the suffrage movement — albeit the more radical wing — was to lobby directly with the representatives who would cast their votes for or against the suffrage amendment. As the Club Movement grew in numbers and strength at the end of the nineteenth century and beginning of the twentieth, the task of many members was to confer with public officials over issues of interest to their clubs. Contacts with public officials were not limited to the organizationally active women. Histories of urban political machines tell us of the machine leaders and lieutenants distributing Thanksgiving turkeys to immigrant housewives and helping them with the problems of their sick and truant children; from the point of view of women's history the important fact is that these women went to these officials to seek solutions to their problems and that the machines were responsive — even if for purely practical political reasons.

One of the most important strategies of women's political influence has been the use of protest, demonstration, and boycott. Michael Lipsky points out that protest is perhaps the only effective strategy for political influence among resource-poor groups; this description certainly fits women throughout most of their history. Protest is a means of communication. It is an attempt to make others aware of social problems and to influence the influential with numbers, unusual noise or acts and, often, implicit threats of violence.[19] From the time of the women's protest against the Oppian law in Rome, women have often found public demonstrations the only channel available to them. Boycotts of consumer goods, from tea during the American Revolution to silk in World War II to the various boycotts of meat, sugar, coffee, grapes, and lettuce in the 1970s, depend upon the cooperation and, often, leadership of women. The history of American demonstrations for peace and civil rights serves as well as a major part of the history of American women. The first public demonstrations at the White House gates were suffrage demonstrations. The first — and presumably the last — force feeding of prisoners participating in hunger strikes were perpetuated against these same suffragists.

Demonstrations are political acts of last resort in the United States. They have been considered a particular affront when women were the demonstrators. Demonstrations by women violate most of the norms of femininity. They often involve women in public unaccompanied by men, they cannot be accomplished through the use of soft-spoken, timid, deferent female language, and even the silent vigil, candlelight parade, or potential martyrdom of civil disobedience are acts of assertiveness and force. Furthermore, there is continuing evidence that even the most aggressive man finds facing a group of women an intimidating prospect. As Lyndon Johnson supposedly said, "I like women singly but I am afraid of them in groups."[20] Political protest is probably the most "unladylike" strategy of political communication.

We will begin our empirical investigation of political participation by analyzing the effects of women's roles on (1) their attempts to "talk to any people and try to show them why they should vote one way or the other" (Talk), (2) whether they ever contacted any public official (Public Officials) or wrote a letter to an editor of a newspaper or magazine to give an opinion (Editors), and (3) whether they ever took part in a "demonstration, protest march, or sit-in" (Protest). One feature of the analysis must be pointed out before discussing the results. Panel analysis is employed in this chapter as it was previously, but the choice of a 1965 baseline variable requires more justification than those used earlier. In the analysis presented in Chapter 5, a variable identical to that serving as the dependent variable is present in the 1965 data in each case. This is not true for the participation data, thus making the choice of a 1965 baseline more problematic. The high school seniors' participation in mass media use and their reports on talking about politics with their families was ruled out; despite low parent-child correlations in the original study[21] it is still questionable how much political behavior within a family by children is a reflection of the children's own predilections versus those of their parents. Participation in high school elections and similar political activities in school was also ruled out as too problematic. The 1965 baseline was therefore constructed from responses to two questions. The first asked for the students' level of interest in politics, the second asked them to anticipate the amount of political activity in which they would engage as adults.[22] The responses were added together to create an index which should provide a measure of earlier levels of interest in politics as well as capture effectively the effects of anticipatory socialization, thus leaving us with the ability to get a clear picture of the effects of adult roles on political participation.

Taking the sample as a whole, women's roles have no significant direct effects on women's attempts to talk to others in an effort to influence their votes or on their attempts to contact public officials (Table 6:1). Rather, these two acts of participation are based in part on prior levels of activism and education. Forty-two percent of the women reported talking to others, 29 percent reported contacting public officials. In contrast, very few women wrote letters to editors of newspapers (5 percent), but in this case privatization does serve as an inhibitor to communication, while education virtually disappears as a predictor. The difference between the first two forms of communication and the third lies in the audience; when one writes a letter to the editor of a public periodical the point is not usually to contact an editor, it is to make a public statement. Thus privatization has as depressing an effect on public letter writing as prior tendency toward activism has a positive effect.

Table 6:1
Determinants of Women's Participation in Four Types of
Political Communication

Determinants	Talk	Public Officials	Editors	Protest
1965 Activism	.17*	.13*	.09*	.06
Education	.20*	.22*	.06	.15*
Marriage	.02	−.01	−.05	−.16*
Motherhood	−.05	.04	−.05	.00
Homemaking	−.06	−.02	.02	.00
Privatization	−.05	−.05	−.09*	−.19*
R^2	.12	.09	.04	.12
(N)	(663)	(652)	(653)	(663)

Note. Unless otherwise specified, all data are drawn from the 1973 wave of the survey, entries are standardized regression coefficients throughout this chapter.
*$p < .05$.

Participation in demonstrations is the most public, assertive, and "hardest" act of communication of all and it is also the act of political communication most dependent upon women's roles. Protest participation differs from the other forms of communication in that it appears unrelated to prior activism; rather, it is dependent upon education, marital status, and privatization. The explanation for the effect of education on protest is fairly clear cut. Beside the usual boost education has been shown to give participation, the women who went to college would have had greater opportunities to participate. Protest activities are generally not done alone; the most important resource necessary for a demonstration is a group of people who are willing to join in. College campuses served as constant foci of organizing attempts in the late 1960s and early 1970s. Thus, 33 percent of the college-educated women report participating in demonstrations compared with 9 percent of the high school graduates. Perhaps the most intriguing aspect of the direct relationship between education and protest participation is that it is not stronger.

Marriage has approximately the same effect on protest activity as it does on political trust. Once again we have evidence that marriage is related to respectful relations with authorities; as we shall see, marriage has no direct bearing on any form of conventional participation we shall investigate. Separate analysis shows that political trust is inversely related to protest participation, as others have found, but inclusion of political trust in the regression equation does not significantly decrease the effects of marital status or, for that matter, privatization. Considering the relationship between marriage and protest behavior in the context of other adult socialization research, the norms of responsibility and adulthood inherent in marriage might lead people to shun the political activities regarded as essentially irresponsible by much of the public in favor of more conventional acts of participation.

Privatization is also related to protest behavior. Women who believe that "women's place is in the home" are relatively unlikely to make public spectacles of themselves. One might suspect, of course, that privatization is related to protest behavior because the egalitarians would be motivated to participate in feminist demonstrations. In fact, that is not the case here. Only a few of the demonstrators said that they had been involved in women's demonstrations. The vast majority participated only in other types of demonstrations. This finding is particularly interesting in light of turns of events in political participation in the late 1970s and early 1980s. As controversies over abortion policies, the Equal Rights Amendment, homosexuality, and similar issues heated up, the left lost what appeared to be the near exclusive rights to protest activity that they had in the late 1960s. Women's organizations within the new right, parts of which were later labeled "the moral majority," began to mount demonstrations of their own, often in "defense of the family." These demonstrations reveal the complexities of women's participation in politics. Even the women of the "moral majority," sometimes toting and quoting the Bible in their efforts to reinstate traditional family values, seem to leave behind the dictum, "Suffer women not to speak . . . ," at least as long as they are demonstrating support for other traditional values.[23]

Marital status has *direct* effects only on protest behavior, but it also affects the *source of and constraints on* women's political communication, as Table 6:2 shows. A comparison of the effects of education with those of 1965 levels of activism proves very revealing. In the case of the easiest acts of political communication, talking to others, earlier levels of activism remain sources of current participation for both single and married women. Higher education, on the other hand, appears to be a necessary resource for many married women to become involved in these types of influence attempts, while that is not the case for single women. Education also serves as a more important basis for married women's attempts to influence public officials directly than it is for single women. Early predispositions toward activism are significantly related to both married and single women's influence attempts in this regard, but more so for single women.

In the two more public modes of communication, writing letters to editors and participating in demonstrations, part of the source of single women's activities, is the earlier level of activism; this is not true at all for married women. As for education, although college-educated women are more likely to participate in demonstrations than are high school graduates regardless of marital status, married women, who are less likely to participate in the first place, appear to be less encouraged by their education to participate than are single women.

In two cases we find the effects of women's roles themselves vary depending on marital status. Single mothers are inhibited in their attempts to influence others but motherhood does not have a similar effect on married women. Privatization has a significant depressing effect on married women's tendency to write letters to editors of newspapers, while the same is not true for single women.

What do we make of these different effects of marital status? For the more private, or one-to-one contacts (talking, contacting public officials), activism is based at least in part on prior levels of activism, but the added resource of education appears necessary to get married women to become involved. Single mothers may have special constraints on their time and attention that make talking about politics in an effort to influence votes not worth the effort relative to other tasks. On the other hand, motherhood does not inhibit the likelihood that single women will contact public offi-

Table 6:2

Determinants of Women's Participation in Four Types of Political Communication, by Marital Status

Determinants	Talk		Public Officials		Editors		Protest	
	Single	Married	Single	Married	Single	Married	Single	Married
1965 Activism	.20*	.15*	.23*	.09*	.20*	.02	.17*	-.01
Education	.08	.24*	.11	.27*	.06	.07	.24*	.12*
Motherhood	-.16*	-.03	.07	.02	-.05	-.05	.02	.00
Homemaking	—	-.06	—	-.01	—	.02	—	-.02
Privatization	-.04	-.05	-.06	-.05	-.06	-.11*	-.25*	-.17*
R²	.09	.13	.08	.10	.07	.03	.19	.06
(N)	(186)	(477)	(183)	(469)	(184)	(469)	(186)	(477)

Note. For further explanation, see Table 6:1.
*p < .05.

cials. This difference in the effect of motherhood should not be a surprise given the numbers of single mothers who must be in contact with public officials about child support and AFDC payments.

As for the more public acts of communication (letters to editors and protest), participation is to some degree an extension of prior levels of activism for single women but not at all for married women. A high level of education is not essential for becoming a letter writer for either single or married women, but privatization serves to inhibit married women. Turning to the most public and assertive mode of communication, protest behavior, we find that privatization blocks participation of both married and single women, and that marriage is antithetical enough to protest so that protest bears no relation to prior activism among married women and college education does not do as much to activate them as it does for single women.

We have seen that women's roles have some effect on their attempts to use political communication for the purpose of influencing others, but we have not yet explored the composition of the networks within which women may exert influence. Much has been made of the limitations women's roles place on their contacts and communication networks.[24] A number of observers stress the parochialism of women's lives, owing primarily to their enclosure within the home and the lack of access to a wide range of social contacts.[25]

Lynn and Flora have written that one of the key factors in the political socialization process of adult women is the constraint on communication imposed by women's most common roles.[26] They discuss four types of interaction networks, including those that are centered on the child, the job, voluntary organizations, and the media. Interaction networks provide significant others through which people develop self-identity and they provide sources of information and objects of influence.

Very often — especially in the past — becoming a mother closed off the job network (and perhaps others) and increased the importance of the child-centered network, which is likely to be the least political. Since communication networks are interrelated, a constraint on one, particularly if it is the occupational network, is likely to lead to a constraint on others. The constriction of interaction networks by gender roles structures is directly related to the problem of female privatization.

The social networks of housewives and especially those with young children are relatively limited in scope and, as Helena Lopata points out, in character.[27] In an analysis of neighboring among housewives, Lopata finds a pattern of cycles of neighboring. During the early period of marriage, before the birth of children, couples tend to be involved with themselves and "with social roles such as school and work, which are not likely to be located in the immediate vicinity." They tend to live in a neighborhood they plan to leave once the husband is settled into his job or when the family starts to expand. In this first phase, neighboring interactions are limited, more distant interactions are more frequent.

The second phase in neighboring occurs with the birth of the first child. "Most wife-mothers remain at home with the infant, suddenly cut off from adult companionship during most of the day. . . . [Many] turn to their neighborhood in a search for compatible women in similar life circumstances."[28] Although women's communication networks become geographically limited, we might not assume that this limitation will reduce women's political *interactions,* including influence attempts. Lopata provides some evidence that political interaction will be reduced. Neighboring serves a very specific purpose for these women: it satisfies the need for social interaction. Lopata paints a picture of a very delicate balance of needs and potential problems. On the one hand, women need social contacts. On the other, the neighborhood is a socio-ecological system; hostilities and competition may develop, contacts may pass the point of comfort and become entrapments. The result is that neighboring tends to be ritualized and rule-laden. Political conversation — particularly if the purpose is to influence — may be outside the bounds of the ritual, too dangerous to the well-being and maintenance of the social system.[29]

When the women in this study reported on their attempts to influence others, who were the objects of their communications? Were these contacts shaped by the women's gender roles as prior research suggests they should be? The women who said they had talked to others to try to influence their votes were asked to whom they had talked and were offered a choice of family, friends, or someone at work. The responses were analyzed in two ways; first, to determine whether roles limited the number of types of contacts women made (none, one, two, or all three), and second, to assess the effects of roles on use of each type of network. Taking the sample as a whole, privatization constrains the number of networks within which women engage in political influence (Table 6:3). Although marital status does not itself affect the number of communication networks, it does alter the effects of the other variables on women's contacts. Again we find that the effects of earlier levels of activism and education vary depending on whether a woman is married or not. Among single women, who show the greatest number of contacts, prior levels of activism are more important than they are for married women. In contrast, education is a more important factor in stimulating married women to use different networks. This is particularly true among homemakers, who appear involved in the least number of networks.

Table 6:3
Determinants of the Number of Communication Networks Used, by Marital and Employment Status

Determinants	Total	Single	Married Employed	Married Homemakers	Total Married
1965 Activism	.12*	.18*	.10	.09	.09
Education	.17*	.05	.15*	.30*	.21*
Marriage	−.03	—	—	—	—
Motherhood	.00	−.14	−.01	.14*	.05
Homemaking	−.09	—	—	—	−.11*
Privatization	−.09*	−.09	−.10	−.10	−.10*
R²	.10	.08	.06	.13	.10
Mean # Acts (of three)	0.81	1.02	0.89	0.51	0.73
(N)	(609)	(176)	(251)	(182)	(433)

Note. For further explanation, see Table 6:1.
*p < .05.

The relative importance of motherhood and homemaking for determining the number of women's communication networks is important to note. Prior research is unclear about whether it is motherhood or homemaking that poses more constraints on women's access to channels of interpersonal influence. Very often women's roles are considered in an undifferentiated fashion; women with children are thought of as *homemakers* with children. Lynn and Flora provide a partial exception.[30] Their sample of mothers includes employed women as well as homemakers; they point out that both groups of women find children a constraint on their social interaction. Their empirical investigation of networks for political communication, however, focuses primarily on neighborhood interaction.

The results of this analysis reveal homemaking as the culprit. Homemakers are, by and large, cut off from the workplace as a channel through which to exert influence, thus reducing the number of possible networks. The reason for the clarity of the effects of homemaking vs. motherhood goes beyond this obvious point, however. As we shall see presently, homemaking restricts communication through other networks as well. In addition, Table 6:3 shows that among homemakers, motherhood actually increases the number of political contacts women make, a point which recalls the effects of children on homemakers' interest in national and international politics. As we have seen, relatively few homemakers are childless. As the employment rate among women approaches the majority mark (and a clear majority of women without preschool children are now employed), it is becoming increasingly true that women need a reason to "stay home," much as women once needed a reason to go to work. That reason, of course, is usually the presence of children, especially small children. Women who are homemakers without reasons of motherhood or disability are, in a sense, the most privatized of all. Moreover, Lynn and Flora show that the communication networks of homemaking mothers of little children may be limited to interaction with neighbors with children over issues concerning motherhood.[31] Even these channels are not particularly available to childless homemakers. As many young women have discovered, there are few social situations as uneasy as those encountered by the young childless woman involved in a discussion with a group of young mothers. Such discussions return repeatedly to comparisons of the experiences of motherhood, often in a manner that marks the childless woman as inexperienced, inexpert, one not fully grown up yet; in short, the deviant. Motherhood may contribute to the character of communication networks, but it is the occupational choice of homemaking that is the more direct constraint.

Further evidence of the effects of roles on channels of influence is provided by analysis of the specific targets of influence reported by the women (Table 6:4). It is immediately apparent that single mothers are very restricted in their influence attempts. Single childless women are more active overall, and more likely to use each network than are single mothers. Motherhood does not have quite such devastating effects on married women, although married mothers are much less likely to influence co-workers, primarily because many of these mothers are homemakers. It is clear that motherhood itself is not solely responsible for restricting specific channels of influence; married women without children are more restricted in each category than are single childless women.

Table 6:4
Effects of Marriage and Motherhood in Determining Targets of
Influence Attempts (percent citing each target)

Target	Single		Married	
	Childless	Mother	Childless	Mother
None	51	72	63	67
Family	34	17	26	26
Friends	43	22	31	27
Co-Workers	36	17	27	13
(N)	(145)	(36)	(200)	(245)

Homemaking limits not only one of the networks available to women, but all of them (Table 6:5). Single women and employed wives are relatively similar in the types of networks they use as influence. In contrast, homemakers are least likely to use each network for political influence and especially, they are least likely to exert political influence on friends. This result is consistent with Lynn and Flora's suggestion that homemaker mothers are particularly likely to avoid straining personal relations with friends by keeping their interactions depoliticized.

To conclude this discussion of women's roles and political communication, it is clear that women's domestic roles restrict their ability to exert political influence, even at the interpersonal level. The more public and assertive a form of political influence, the more constraining traditional roles are. Domesticity is depoliticizing at all levels, however. Although women are freer to express themselves than they ever were, women's roles continue to restrict that expression if it is intended to be politically instrumental.

Table 6:5

Effects of Marital and Employment Status in Determining Targets
of Influence Attempts (percent citing target)

Target	Single	Married Employed	Married Homemakers
None	55	58	74
Family	31	29	21
Friends	39	34	21
Co-Workers	32	27	9
(N)	(181)	(257)	(188)

Electoral Activity

Electoral activity has received widespread attention by people
interested in women's political participation. When women were
first brought into the electorate, differences in turnout were substantial. As Charles Merriam and Harold Gosnell showed in their
pioneering volume, *Nonvoting,* many women refrained from casting ballots because they simply did not think it was their place to
do so.[32] As Chapter 2 reported, by taking the populations of women
and men as a whole, we find that turnout rates have increased and
sex differentials have decreased over the last sixty years. We also
saw, however, that small sex differences persist and that there is
no evidence for uniform progress over the last thirty years.

Although electoral participation, including voting, is often taken
as the major indicator of women's progress in politics, research findings are inconclusive. First, considering voting, *The American Voter*
suggests that the presence of small children inhibited women's turnout in the elections of the 1950s.[33] After controlling for age, region,
education, and income, Susan Welch finds that homemaking
depressed female turnout in 1968 and 1972 (although not in 1952),
but motherhood did not.[34] Using somewhat different techniques,
Raymond Wolfinger and Steven Rosenstone found no differences
between homemakers and employed women in 1972, but they did
find that marriage encourages turnout among both men and
women.[35] Hansen, Franz, and Netemeyer-Mays found a small but
nonsignificant relationship between our indicator of privatization
and turnout in 1968 and 1972.[36]

Turning to campaign activity other than voting, prior research proves no more clear. Kristi Andersen's analysis of elections from 1952 to 1972 suggests that employment outside the home encourages participation, although she also notes that other measures of class (including husband's occupation) yield the same results.[37] She also finds that privatization decreases participation in 1972, but particularly among employed women. Welch's analysis shows that employment encouraged women to attend meetings and to attempt to influence others' votes in 1972, and encouraged them to contribute money in 1964.[38] Hansen, Franz, and Netemeyer-Mays found that privatization decreased the number of campaign activities in which women were engaged in 1972.[39]

Seventy percent of the women in this survey voted in 1972. Despite the "ease" of voting (prior activism is apparently unrelated to turnout), women's roles serve as factors in turnout (Table 6:6). As we have found before, marital and employment status have no direct effects on participation, but they do help determine the effects of other resources and roles on turnout. Education promotes turnout among married women (especially those who are employed) but not among single women. Motherhood decreases turnout as Campbell, Converse, Miller, and Stokes suggest, but particularly among single women and, we might add, among married women who are employed ($p < .06$). In these cases we can observe how the demands of single motherhood or the double burden of job and motherhood restrict other nondomestic activities. Privatization has no discernible effect on turnout, as Hansen et al. found.

If gender roles have an effect on turnout, we can be fairly sure they also affect women's involvement in campaign activities. In order to assess the relationships between roles and campaign participation we will use a measure of the number of campaign activities in which the women reported participating. These activities include (a) talking to others in an attempt to influence their votes, (b) attending meetings or rallies, (c) wearing a campaign button or displaying a bumpersticker, (d) giving money, and (e) participating in any "other" campaign activity. Forty-three percent of the women did not engage in any of these activities, 26 percent participated in one, 14 percent in two, and 18 percent in three or more. Forty-two percent said they had tried to influence others' votes, 21 percent went to meetings or rallies, 13 percent gave money, 30 percent wore a

Table 6:6

Determinants of Voting Turnout in 1972 Presidential Election,
by Marital and Employment Status

Determinants	Total	Single	Married Employed	Married Housewife	Total Married
1965 Activism	.02	.09	.01	.00	.00
Education	.22*	.01	.33*	.19*	.28*
Marriage	.04	—	—	—	—
Motherhood	-.09*	-.20*	-.11	.03	-.07
Homemaking	.01	—	—	—	.04
Privatization	.03	.04	-.04	.09	.02
R²	.06	.05	.15	.04	
(N)	(650)	(183)	(272)	(195)	(467)

Note. For further explanation, see Table 6:1.
*p < .05.

Table 6:7

Determinants of Number of Campaign Activities in Which
Women Participated

Determinants	Total	Single	Married Employed	Married Homemaker	Total Married
1965 Activism	.21*	.26*	.22*	.17*	.20*
Education	.20*	.13	.21*	.21*	.21*
Marriage	.01	—	—	—	—
Motherhood	-.07	-.19*	-.02	-.06	-.03
Homemaking	-.05	—	—	—	-.05
Privatization	-.08*	-.05	-.06	-.14*	-.10*
R²	.15	.16	.13	.13	.14
Mean # Acts (of five)	1.21	1.41	1.32	.90	1.14
(N)	(661)	(186)	(227)	(198)	(475)

Note. For further explanation, see Table 6:1.
*p < .05.

button or displayed a bumpersticker, and 16 percent had been
involved in other ways. Table 6:7 shows the effects of roles on campaign participation and includes the mean number of activities in
each category.

For the women as a group, privatization is the only role variable with significant effects on campaign participation. This relationship is accounted for primarily by married homemakers, who are relatively inactive in the first place. Privatization is particularly likely to depress their level of participation. In addition, single mothers are at a clear disadvantage in electoral participation. Research on family roles shows that married women have little enough assistance in taking care of their children; the burden of being a single mother leaves little spare energy or time for campaign activism. Single mothers engaged in an average of .69 campaign activities compared with .93 activities among married mothers, 1.37 among childless married women, and 1.57 among childless single women.

Once again, employment does not appear to have direct effects on women's participation. One of the primary ways through which people may become involved in electoral campaigns is through the political party; as many people have noted, women, including homemakers, are particularly active in giving their time to volunteer work for their parties. Thus employment itself does not appear to promote campaign participation. Employment does, however, make a difference in the effects of the norm of privatization. Homemakers who interpret their roles as particularly private are much less likely to become engaged in campaigning than are homemakers who do not. The less privatized homemakers may serve as the well known troops of stamp lickers, telephone callers, and canvassers. The critical factor does not seem to be employment per se, but the interpretation of their roles.

Community Participation

In the past few years, an increased amount of attention has been paid to women's involvement in community politics and problems for a number of reasons. First, there has been a growth in interest in and support for community activism and voluntarism since the middle of the 1960s. Many public policies aiming at the local level began to depend upon or require local and neighborhood citizen action and involvement. One of the watchwords of local politics and, especially, reform became "citizen participation." These new developments spawned an explosion of academic interest in voluntary citizen action, books and journals devoted to the subject, and, in 1971, the establishment of the Nixon-created National Center for Voluntary Action.

More specific to the case of women, two developments have been of interest. On the academic side, as women's studies scholars began to study the contemporary and historical political roles of women, they found that women's participation and influence has been seriously underestimated, largely because women's accomplishments and involvement have been ignored for the most part or labelled "nonpolitical." The League of Women Voters, for example, is one of the largest political organizations in the United States outside the political parties; it has been devoted to citizen education and mobilization for over a half century, since its inception as a transformation of the National American Women's Suffrage Association. If this organization is mentioned at all in the literature of political studies, it is rarely treated in a substantive manner. References to women's historical and contemporary involvement in social services, redistribution, and a wide range of on-going and *ad hoc* community organizations are scant. Often women's community involvement is wiped nearly clean of its political import and discussed instead as a good thing for middle class housewives to do with spare time, or as essentially social rather than political activities.[40]

On the practical political side, as women became aware of the special problems faced by women and the slowness of response in the late 1960s and 1970s, there developed renewed effort to organize women both to lobby and to solve their own problems within their communities. As a result, by the late 1970s communities of every type and size across the country witnessed a wide range of social services and organizations established by women and for women. We should take note, however, that some feminists have been less than fully optimistic about the significance of women's community participation for the expansion of women's influence and political integration. Women have, after all, participated in large numbers for a long time; their impact is largely forgotten from one decade to the next. Also, women's impact has, in many senses, been greatest when they worked through women's organizations. Although united action on the part of women has been important, such segregation has also made it relatively easy for the male political and academic worlds to underplay and ignore them. Another criticism of women's community activity is that although women have been relatively successful at establishing their own services and providing for their needs through private organizations with little assistance from the private sector, such organizations may take the burden off the public sector to provide what are essentially public goods. Finally, many people have charged that much of the community work women do involves the donation of services that would be reimbursed were they men working in men's organizations. The experience of many women returning to employment in midlife underscores the problem. Many women who have spent years performing volunteer services have found that when they apply for jobs that require similar types of skills to those they used in their volunteer work, their years of voluntarism are not counted as job experiences or training because their previous experience had never been valued in dollars. Women, many people charge, are conned into devaluing themselves by working in female channels of volunteer service work rather than seeking employment.

The women in this study were asked whether they had worked with others in an attempt to solve a community problem. Twenty-five percent said they had. Preliminary analysis showed that motherhood had very different effects on community participation depending upon the educational attainment of the women. Having children appears to boost community participation among high school graduates and depress community participation among college-educated women. In the former group 9 percent of the childless women and 24 percent of the mothers report having participated in community action, compared with 35 percent of the childless women and 24 percent of the mothers who are college educated. As Table 6:8 shows, these are significant direct effects. Although the nature of these data do not allow full exploration of the reasons, some suggestions are possible. The relationship between motherhood and participation can be viewed in a number of ways. Of particular interest here are two contradictory possibilities. First, motherhood can be seen as consuming time, energy, and attention that might be devoted otherwise to politics. This would be particularly true of mothers of preschoolers. Alternatively, motherhood can be seen as a motivation to participate in local community affairs, especially those revolving around education and other child-related concerns. Recent analysis by M. Kent Jennings shows that the presence of school-aged children seems to have a positive effect on

women's propensity to participate in local school politics and a negative effect on their propensity to participate in nationally-oriented
politics, particularly among women under thirty.[41]

Table 6:8
Determinants of Participation in
Community, by Education

Determinants	No College	College
1965 Activism	.11	.09
Marriage	.00	.07
Motherhood	.24*	-.12*
Homemaking	-.09	.00
Privatization	-.03	.03
R^2	.07	.02
(N)	(281)	(380)

Note. For further explanation, see Table 6:1.
*$p < .05$.

The high school graduates tended to marry and have children
at a younger age than did the college-educated women, as is the
case nationally. Does the relatively high proportion of school-aged
children among the high school graduates account for the community activism of the high-school-educated mothers? It appears
not; the participation rates of mothers with preschoolers and those
with school-aged children is very similar, especially among the high
school graduates. In that group 25 percent of the mothers with only
preschoolers reported helping to solve a community problem compared with 24 percent of those with at least one older child. The
figures are 26 percent and 20 percent, respectively, for college-
educated women.

Unfortunately, small numbers make it very difficult to go very
far in tracing the relationship between motherhood and community
participation, although the data provide some further suggestion.
The women who said they had participated in community affairs
were asked to report on the specific circumstances of their involvement. Of the 107 college-educated women who claimed to have participated in community problem-solving, 29 percent mentioned
youth-oriented activism. In the case of the 45 high school graduates
who reported becoming active, 42 percent mentioned youth-oriented

activities. The tentative conclusion we may reach about community activism and women's roles revolves around class differences in motivations for and restrictions on women's involvement. For college-educated women, having children creates demands on their time and energy which serves to depress their level of local activism at least slightly. When the women with less education participate in community affairs, the focus of their activism is more likely to have a traditional "women's focus" on children and youth in any case than is true for college-educated women. For the high-school-educated women, having children may help integrate them into the local political community by focusing their attention even more on getting involved in community problems centering on children, regardless of their own children's ages. Also, it must be remembered that the college-educated women are involved in a wider range of political activities of all types in the first place. It appears that while motherhood may force the college-educated women selectively to "cut back" in their political activism, motherhood may be a boost to integration into the active life of at least the local political community for the high school graduates. This is the third indication we have had that in some circumstances motherhood may have a positive effect on women's political integration.

Conclusion: Integration and Influence

The strategies women use to try to make the political system work for them depend in part on what types of gender roles they accept and perform. The strategies for political action they choose are partly contingent upon whether they are single or married, employed or homemakers, childless or mothers. The fact that there is a relationship between private and public roles is not necessarily bad in and of itself. But as we saw in both the previous chapter and in this one, the private roles women are expected to perform as adults promote political marginality. In effect, women who establish families and take them as their central concerns in the early years of their adulthood (as, we might add, they were trained to do) delay or restrict the possibility of becoming fully effective members of the political system.

Two important questions about participation and influence must remain unanswered here. The first concerns the effects of women's roles on the potential for elite participation. Although these data do not provide the opportunity to assess the effects of women's adult roles on political ambition and the potential for more influential participatory acts, other research suggests we may view political participation, from casting a ballot or talking to others all the way up to running for national office, as a ladder on which each successive step women might take depends upon their gender roles and ideology. Even among highly politically active women, political ambition and attempts to gain influence through obtaining political office are contingent upon whether one is married, a mother, a homemaker, or accepts the traditional existing ideology of privatization.[42]

The other unanswered question concerns the impact of women's participation. We have looked only at whether different strategies of political action are contingent upon women's private roles. We have not, and cannot here, examine the results of women's activism. The research on women and communication, including political communication, however, suggests that the battle does not lie only in making women free to act. It also lies in making women free to be influential.

NOTES

1. Susan Hansen, Linda Franz, and Margaret Netemeyer-Mays, "Women's Political Participation and Policy Preferences," *Social Science Quarterly* 56 (Mar., 1976), 101.
2. The literature on voter rationality is extensive and, to the uninitiated, unreadable for the most part. For a delightful summary of the problem, see Paul E. Meehl, "The Selfish Voter Paradox and the Thrown-Away Vote Argument," *American Political Science Review* 71 (Mar., 1977), 11-30.
3. Eleanor Maccoby and Carol Jacklin, *The Psychology of Sex Differences* (Stanford: Stanford University Press, 1974).
4. On these differences in conversational styles, see Kay Deaux, *The Behavior of Women and Men* (Monterey, Calif.: Wadsworth Publishing, 1976), Chapter VI; Fred L. Strodtbeck and Richard O. Mann, "Sex Role Differences in Jury Deliberations," *Sociometry* 19 (1956), 3-11; Fred L. Strodtbeck, R. M. James, and C. Hawkins, "Social Status in Jury Deliberation," *American Sociological Review* 22 (1957), 713-19; M. E. Shaw and O. Sadler, "Interaction Patterns in Heterosexual Dyads Varying in Degree of Intimacy," *Journal of Social Psychology* 66 (1965), 345-51; W. F. Kenkel, "Differentiation in Family Deci-

sion-Making," *Sociology and Social Research* 42 (1957), 18-25; James March, "Husband-Wife Interaction Over Political Issues," *Public Opinion Quarterly* 17 (Winter, 1953-54), 461-470; Marlaine E. Lockheed, "Conceptualizing Sex as a Status Characteristic: Applications to Leadership Training Strategies," *Journal of Social Issues* 32 (Summer, 1976), 111-24.

5. Edward Megargee, "Influence of Sex Roles on the Manifestation of Leadership," *Journal of Applied Psychology* 53 (1969), 377-82.

6. For summary and analysis of male-female bargaining styles that supports Megargee's conclusions, see Virginia Sapiro, "Sex and Games: On Oppression and Rationality," *British Journal of Political Science* 9 (1979), 385-408.

7. Kenkel, "Differentiation in Family Decision-Making"; March, "Husband-Wife Interaction over Political Issues"; Deaux, *The Behavior of Women and Men*, p. 95.

8. Bertram H. Raven, R. Centers, and A. Rodriguez, "The Bases of Conjugal Power," in R. E. Cromwell and D. H. Olson, eds., *Power in Families* (New York: Wiley, 1975).

9. Raven, Centers, and Rodriguez, "The Bases of Conjugal Power"; Paula Johnson, "Women and Power: Toward a Theory of Effectiveness," *Journal of Social Issues* 32 (Summer, 1976), 99-110.

10. Irene Frieze et al., *Women and Sex Roles: A Social Psychological Perspective* (New York: W.W. Norton, 1978), p. 316.

11. For reviews of the differences, see Diana Warshay, "Sex Differences in Language Style," in C. Safilios-Rothschild, ed., *Toward a Sociology of Women* (Lexington: Xerox Corporation, 1972), pp. 3-9; Mary Ritchie Key, *Male/Female Language* (Metuchen, N.J.: Scarecrow Press, 1975); Robin Lakoff, *Language and Women's Place* (New York: Harper and Row, 1975); Nancy Henley and Barrie Thorne, eds., *Language and Sex* (Rowley: Newbury House, 1975).

12. Nancy Henley, *Body Politics* (Englewood Cliffs: Prentice-Hall, 1977).

13. Janet K. Boles, *The Politics of the Equal Rights Amendment: Conflict and the Decision Process* (New York: Longman, 1979), p. 114.

14. *Ibid.*

15. Bonnie Cook-Freeman, "Women's Unwanted Liberation: A Case Study of a Paradox?", paper delivered at the Annual Meeting of the Midwest Political Science Association, Chicago, 1979, p. 25.

16. *Ibid.*, p. 26.

17. Naomi Lynn and Cornelia Flora, "Motherhood and Political Participation: The Changing Sense of Self," *Journal of Political and Military Sociology* 1 (Spring, 1973), 91-103.

18. Linda Grant de Pauw, *Founding Mothers: Women of America in the Revolutionary Era* (Boston: Houghton Mifflin, 1975), pp. 166-67.

19. Michael Lipsky, "Protest as a Political Resource," *American Political Science Review* 62 (Dec., 1968), 1144-58. For a recent book that reviews the literature on political protest and provides an excellent

empirical study of protest behavior in Britain, see Alan Marsh, *Protest and Political Consciousness* (Beverly Hills: Sage, 1977).

20. Boles, *The Politics of the Equal Rights Amendment*, p. 113.
21. M. Kent Jennings and Richard G. Niemi, *The Political Character of Adolescence* (Princeton: Princeton University Press, 1974), pp. 300-301.
22. The two questions were:

    > Some people seem to think about what's going on in government and public affairs most of the time, whether there's an election going on or not. Others aren't that interested. Would you say you follow what's going on in government and public affairs most of the time, some of the time, only now and then, or hardly at all?

    > Looking ahead to the one time when you are on your own, what about actual participation in public affairs and politics. Do you think you will be very active, somewhat active, or not very active in these matters?

23. On antifeminist movements and political strategies see Boles, "The Politics of the Equal Rights Amendment"; David W. Brady and Kent L. Tedin, "Ladies in Pink: Religion and Political Ideology in the Anti-ERA Movement," *Social Science Quarterly* 56 (Mar., 1976), 564-75; Cook-Freeman, "Women's Unwanted Liberation"; Pam Conover, Steve Coombs, and Virginia Gray, "The Attitudinal Roots of Single-Issue Politics: The Case of 'Women's Issues,' " paper prepared for the Annual Meeting of the American Political Science Association, Washington, D.C., 1980.
24. Especially Lynn and Flora, "Motherhood and Political Participation"; Helena Lopata, *Occupation: Housewife* (New York: Oxford, 1971); Mirra Komarovsky, *Blue Collar Marriage* (New York: Random House, 1967).
25. Especially Robert Lane, *Political Life* (New York: Free Press, 1959).
26. Lynn and Flora, "Motherhood and Political Participation."
27. Lopata, *Occupation: Housewife.*
28. *Ibid.*, p. 245.
29. See also Lynn and Flora, "Motherhood and Political Participation."
30. *Ibid.*
31. *Ibid.*
32. Charles Merriam and Harold Gosnell, *Nonvoting* (Chicago: University of Chicago Press, 1924).
33. Angus Campbell, Philip Converse, Warren Miller, and Donald Stokes, *The American Voter* (New York: Wiley, 1964).
34. Susan Welch, "Women as Political Animals? A Test of Some Explanations for Male-Female Political Participation Differences," *American Journal of Political Science* 21 (Nov., 1977), 711-30.
35. Raymond Wolfinger and Steven Rosenstone, *Who Votes?* (New Haven: Yale University Press, 1980).

36. Hansen, Franz, and Netemeyer-Mays, "Women's Political Participation and Policy Preferences."
37. Kristi Andersen, "Working Women and Political Participation, 1952-1972," *American Journal of Political Science* 19 (Aug., 1975), 439-53.
38. Welch, "Women as Political Animals?"
39. Hansen, Franz, and Netemeyer-Mays, "Women's Political Participation and Policy Preferences."
40. For some works on volunteer action and community participation, see Constance Smith and Anne Friedman, *Voluntary Associations: Perspectives on the Literature* (Cambridge: Harvard University Press, 1972).
41. M. Kent Jennings, "Another Look at the Life Cycle and Political Participation," *American Journal of Political Science* 23 (Nov., 1979), 755-71.
42. Virginia Sapiro, "Public Costs of Private Commitments or Private Costs of Public Commitments: Family Roles *versus* Political Ambition," *American Journal of Political Science* 26 (May, 1982); Virginia Sapiro and Barbara G. Farah, "New Pride and Old Prejudice: Political Ambition and Role Orientations among Female Partisan Elites," *Women and Politics* 1 (Spring, 1980), 13-36. Some research shows that male participation is not affected by private familial roles in the same way as is women's either at the mass or elite level. See Jennings "Another Look at the Life Cycle"; and Sapiro, "Public Costs of Private Commitments or Private Costs of Public Commitments."

CHAPTER 7

The Substance of Politics: "Women's Points of View"

> I am occasionally desired by congenital
> imbeciles and the editors of magazines to say
> something about the writing of detective fiction
> "from the woman's point of view." To such
> demands one can only say, "Go away and
> don't be silly. You might as well ask what is
> the female angle on an equilateral triangle."
>
> In the old days it used to be said that women
> were unsuited to sit in Parliament because . . .
> their views would be cramped and domestic —
> in short, "the woman's point of view." Now
> that they *are* in Parliament, people claim
> disappointment: they vote like other people
> with their party and have contributed nothing
> to speak of from "the woman's point of view."
> . . . It looks as though somebody was trying to
> have things both ways at once. . . .[1]

Not all observers of women's political roles have thought of those
who ask about the "woman's point of view" as congenital imbeciles.
The concern over such a phenomenon is longstanding, reaching back
to the days of speculation over the effects of the proposal to grant
women the right to vote. In the pre- and immediate post-suffrage
period, the political parties took the possibility of a woman's block
vote seriously enough to trip over each other in an effort to cater
to the woman's point of view.[2] Although it quickly became apparent
that only in the rarest instances would women be in enough agreement to make some group will felt, both scholarly and public
observers of women in more recent years see a women's interest
or point of view in politics. What is this view and what is its source?

Conventional wisdom on the subject in political science has generally relied upon the results of four studies from the late 1950s. In the first cross-national empirical study of women and politics, Maurice Duverger observed disproportionate numbers of women's votes for conservative and religious parties.[3] The authors of *The American Voter* noted a slight tendency for women to vote disproportionately Republican.[4] In *Political Life*, Robert Lane focuses on the special interests and underlying values of women. He noted that women "have special reasons to be interested in problems of price control, housing, zoning, education, playgrounds, prevention of war, and so forth. . . ."[5] In one of the most often quoted passages in his discussion of women, Lane offered moralism and idealism as the underlying values of the woman's point of view.[6] In addition he agreed with David Riesman's observation that women tend to "limit attention to the superficial and irrelevant aspects of politics."[7] Finally, Samuel Stouffer suggested that female moralism in politics is the source of the relatively high degree of intolerance he observed among women.[8]

Results from one of the items in a 1972 Harris study of women's roles demonstrates how deeply embedded notions of a woman's interest in politics are in the American public.[9] In that study a national sample of American women and men (N=4020) was asked, "When it comes to (issue named), do you feel that women in public office could do a better job than men, a worse job than men, or just as good a job as men in public office?" The opinions of the combined sample of women and men are displayed in Table 7:1. Over half the respondents felt women would be better at issues dealing with children and the family, the arts, and the interests of the consumer while over half felt men would be better at issues involving big business and the military. In addition the public sees a marked advantage for women in handling problems of poverty, health, education, and peace. They see an advantage for men in dealing with demonstrations and international diplomacy. Some of the finer distinctions made by the public are worth noting. Women are thought to be relatively good at dealing with education but bad at dealing with student demonstrations, good at coping with problems of poverty, education, and environment but bad at solving the urban crisis. Most striking of all, women are given good marks for working for peace, but very low marks for dealing with Vietnam, diplomacy, and directing the military.

Table 7:1

Public Images of Relative Issue-Expertise of Women and Men

Issues	Women Better (%)	Equal (%)	Men Better (%)	Female Advantage[a] (%)
Dealing with children and family problems	69	27	4	+65
Encouraging the arts	52	42	6	+46
Protecting the interests of the consumer	51	38	11	+40
Assisting the poor	47	44	9	+38
Dealing with health problems	44	48	9	+36
Improving educational system	41	49	10	+31
Working for peace in world	34	53	13	+21
Maintaining honesty and integrity in government	29	57	14	+15
Protecting the environment	31	49	20	+11
Improving justice for minorities	22	59	19	+ 3
Strengthening the economy	22	50	28	− 6
Improving the prison system	26	35	39	−10
Solving the urban crisis	18	54	28	−10
Making decisions on whether or not to go to war	25	38	37	−12
Getting us out of Vietnam	17	53	30	−12
Balancing the federal budget	19	48	33	−14
Dealing with student demonstrators	12	44	32	−20
Conducting diplomatic relations with other countries	15	48	37	−22
Dealing with big business	5	41	54	−49
Directing the military	3	20	77	−74

Source: Louis Harris 1972 Virginia Slims Poll.

[a] "Female advantage" is computed by subtracting the proportion citing men as more competent from the proportion citing women as more competent.

These stereotypes of the "woman's point of view" are easily accounted for as relatively simple extrapolations from women's private, domestic roles to public issues and problems as illustrated in Table 7:2.[10] Despite changes in women's public roles during the course of this century, and especially in recent years, women's primary responsibility and concern is still considered to be the roles and problems of domestic life. As mothers, women are expected to be particularly interested in and expert at promoting policies directly and indirectly affecting child welfare; as homemakers, they are expected to understand and promote consumer welfare and rights.

Table 7:2
Common Extrapolations from Domestic Roles to Political Interests

Domestic Role	Political Interest
Mother	Child welfare: child labor / recreation / environment / morality
	Social welfare
	Education
	Peace
Housekeeper	Civic reform
	Environment
Guardian of domestic tranquility and harmony	Peace
	Arts and culture
Guardian of religion and domestic morality	"Moral" issues
	Education
Consumer	Consumer
Woman	Issues directly affecting the welfare and rights of women

Expectations of women's political views and expertise go beyond specific child-welfare and consumer policies. As the traditional guardians of domestic tranquility and harmony, in their "expressive roles," as Talcott Parsons would say,[11] women are also supposed to be particularly concerned with peace issues as well as the arts and culture. More directly, mothers (as compared with fathers) are supposed to be particularly reluctant to send their sons off to battle.

Of course, World War I posters more often than not featured not the arrow-and-olive-branch-carrying eagle, clearly a masculine image, but rather Miss Liberty, Joan of Arc, or M-O-T-H-E-R. When peace fails, the female images of Liberty, justice, or home may justify battle.

In their capacity as traditional guardians of religion and morality they are expected to bring these values to bear on their consideration of public issues. Part of this moralism, of course, is attributed to women's functions as mothers. In addition, the homemaking role has often been cited as a source of morality; Jane Addams, for example, argued that women could use their housekeeping skills to clean both government and the environment.[12] Many examples of expectations of women's moral housekeeping are available. Finley Peter Dunne had his popular characters, Hennessy and Dooley, engage in the following conversation: " 'I udden't talk to me wife about votin' anny more thin sh'd talk to me about thrimmin' a hat,' said Mr. Hennessy. 'Well,' said Mr. Dooley, 'if she gets a vote maybe she'll thrim it to please ye. Annyhow it won't be a bad thing. What this country needs is voters that knows something about housekeeping.' "[13] Grand allusions to women's state-housekeeping potential were standard elements of turn-of-the-century suffrage rhetoric.

Women's roles at home also lead people to see women not simply as nurturers of their own children, but as nurturers of the world. Women are supposed to be particularly social-welfare-oriented and concerned for the plight of the downtrodden. It is no coincidence that it is a woman who is embossed with the words, "Give me your tired, your poor. . . ."

The problem of a "woman's point of view" is an important one in the context of political integration. The woman's vantage point is supposed to be the view from the kitchen, the view of a privatized person. The existence of such a view, however, raises some problems that are in many ways considerably thornier than those presented by the effects of privatization on psychological resources or political participation. Most people might agree that if women's roles inhibit the development of a feeling of efficacy or the ability to participate where action is necessary, those roles must be changed. But what if we find that women's roles encourage a particular approach to political issues or a special set of values. Is that bad? Not necessarily.

If women are particularly concerned with child-welfare issues because they are mothers, what is the problem? Most feminists would suggest that the problem is not that women are privatized and therefore are concerned with children or wish for the political system to deal with children in a nurturant way. Rather, they would argue that the problem is that the *issue* is privatized. More specifically, the identification of women *rather than* men with the value of nurturance means that those who control public policy are too divorced from a concern for children and see that — as well as many other "women's issues" — as private concerns, inappropriate for government action. Nowhere has this been more obvious than in the issue of federally supported day care. The primary opposition to a national day care system is that day care would take childcare out of the private domain of the family "where it belongs."[14] Thus men, who typically do little to assist in the care of their children, leave women to fend for themselves in caring for the children the two sexes supposedly share.[15]

A second objection to a national day care system reveals more of what is meant by "the woman's point of view." Day care, it is said, is too expensive. "Expense," in public policy terms, is not an absolute measure, it is a relative one. "Too expensive" indicates that a particular policy would require cutting into the funds necessary for another, more preferred policy. It is not necessarily the case that a rejection of day care means that policymakers are either opposed to the care of children or that they do not understand the plight of women who have both jobs and children. Rather, they must choose among competing values in their decisions over the distribution of scarce resources, and they rank other values as more important than government guarantees of care for children. Similarly, the concept of a woman's point of view suggests that particular aspects of women's personality and/or roles make some values more important to them than other values.

What, then, could be wrong with a "woman's point of view"? The answer is, a number of things. First, if issues such as peace, child welfare, moralism, and so forth are truly "women's issues" in the traditional sense, we have cause for concern over the question of why these issues are not as much concerns of men. Second, the idea of a woman's point of view has not simply referred to a simple rank-ordering of values by gender, but to a particular style among women. Women are supposed to be parochial in their preferences, involved in their own concerns without adequate attention to or understanding of alternative points of view and issues. Robert Lane, for example, has argued that women's moralism is due to their "more restricted contacts in society and narrower range of experience [which] may tend to reinforce the view that the values they are familiar with are the only values. . . ." He labels this a "lack of cultural relativism."[16] This type of interpretation of women's political values is very problematic for women. For example, although one female stereotype is that women are particularly peace-oriented and skilled at expressive tasks, this is not taken by most people to mean that we would be better off if women predominated in the State and Defense Departments. Rather, women are thought to be peace-oriented to the exclusion of understanding the complexities and occasional necessities of conflict. Men, on the other hand, may desire peace, but they are considered more rational (i.e., aggressive) in their pursuit of peace. This example demonstrates the irony of the application of the concept "representation" to women. The fact that many people understand women to have a distinct point of view has been part of the justification for *not* including women in a number of types of decision-making posts.

A problem that obstructs the ability to understand the relationship of gender to public opinion is a lack of clarity in the contours of the meaning of a woman's point of view. Although private roles are central to any conception of "women's political attitudes," what part of political thought or opinion those roles influence appears to shift from one discussion to the next. Some people suggest that women's private roles make some issues or policy areas particularly salient to women; that is, women's roles create interest in, for example, child welfare policies. Others seem to suggest that women's roles may be seen as providing or blocking expertise. Here we might argue that, regardless of women's specific opinions, their private roles give them experiences that make them more or less competent to understand and make decisions about particular policy problems.

These distinctions offer further explanations of public views of women's political attitudes. Let us return to the question of women in the State or Defense departments. People may well assume that women are particularly likely to value peace over war, and they might even agree with the value ranking. The problem is that the same people probably feel that women's roles do not give them the expertise to pursue the goal of peace constructively. Even granting that fewer women than men have military or defense experience, we may hazard a guess that many, if not most, people would feel more comfortable with a male Secretary of Defense than with a female of similar background.

Interestingly, female public opinion remains one of the most unexplored areas of women's studies within political science. One of the reasons is that, despite stereotypes to the contrary, very few differences in opinion between men and women have been found in the past. The lack of sex differences, however, still does not put to rest questions of the relationship of adult gender roles to political thought.

Another special problem with analysis of women's political attitudes is confusion over the reported conservatism of women. As will be discussed below, women's conservatism has been attributed to their roles as preservers and transmitters of culture, as well as a fear of risk and change, also derived from their domestic roles. Women's conservatism is often also identified more precisely as a conservative moralistic approach to politics. On the other hand, statements about women's conservatism cannot be easily resolved with claims about women's social welfare attitudes, which are also supposed to be derived from their roles as nurturers. Thus, the image of women's political attitudes fits uneasily into usual understandings of a liberal-conservative continuum.

If the experiences of homemaking, marriage, or motherhood help shape women's political attitudes and values, we should be able to see differences between women who are engaged in these roles and those who are not. Indeed, socialization theory and research increasingly point to adult roles and role assumption as important factors in the development of political values and perspectives.[17] If parochial concern with the home is important in determining women's approach to politics, the more parochial, privatized women should have different values from the other women. The analysis and discussion will focus especially on liberal and conservative attitudes, beginning with self-reported conservatism and continuing with party identification, moralism, and social welfare attitudes.

Self-Reported Conservatism

Explanations of women's conservatism are excellent cases of extrapolation from the private — especially domestic — sphere to the public. As men's lives have become less dominated by ascriptive values over the last few centuries, the lag in women's lives has become more apparent. The traditional ideal pictures women's lives as being more stable and evolutionary; success is based on following a path from girlhood to wifehood and motherhood as prescribed at birth. Success within the latter two stages is judged by the expressive values of preservation and transmission of cultural norms and maintenance of domestic harmony. In contrast, men are supposed to manipulate symbols and resources and achieve and acquire in the public sphere. Whether stated as an instrumental-expressive or an acquisition-preservation dichotomy, women's primary role is the more conservative of the two.[18]

Dependency of women, as fostered by cultural norms, laws, and social institutions, also has conservative implications. Dependency is most clearly institutionalized in the laws and customs of marriage, in which a woman is supposed to rely upon a man to support and protect her. Her well-being depends on the security and stability of this relationship, especially given the lack of support for the "old maid" or divorcee, the lack of job preparation for a woman who has been a housewife, discrimination against women in employment, and the lack of childcare facilities. Even in public pursuits a woman has been supposed to require protection because "her physical structure and a proper discharge of her maternal functions — having in view not merely her own health, but the well-being of the race — justify legislation to protect her from the greed as well as the passion of man."[19] Thus women's dependency and its complement, protection — especially in marriage — may foster a need for security, fear of change, and general conservatism.[20]

The women in this study were asked to place themselves on a liberal-to-conservative continuum.[21] Table 7:3 shows the results of multivariate analysis of the effects of women's roles on conservatism.[22] There is a slight positive relationship between marriage and conservatism and a moderate relationship between privatization and conservatism. Breaking these effects down to zero order relationships, we find that 28 percent of the married women identified themselves as conservative compared with 19 percent of the single women, 30 percent of the married women called themselves liberal compared with 52 percent of the single women. With regard to privatization, 42 percent of those who scored high were conservatives compared with 18 percent of those who scored low. In contrast, 9 percent of those who scored high considered themselves liberals compared with 53 percent of those who scored low.

Table 7:3
Determinants of Self-Reported Conservatism

Determinants	
Education	−.03
Marriage	.12*
Motherhood	.00
Homemaking	.03
Privatization	.31*
R^2	.13
(N)	(510)

Note. Unless otherwise specified, data are drawn from 1973 wave of the survey, entries are standardized regression coefficients throughout the chapter.
*$p < .05$.

This analysis stands in contrast to the common suggestion that it is the "cloistering effects" of homemaking that support conservatism among women. Women who do not have paid employment may have the opportunity to be sheltered (but they usually gain this opportunity only if they are married) and mothers may find themselves thrown into particular concern for order, discipline, and stability, but it appears to be the role of wife or the structure of marriage that has a more direct link to conservatism. Above all, however, it is the ideology of privatization that has the strongest bearing on conservatism.

It would be plausible to object that the indicator of privatization is also an indicator of conservatism and thus that the results of the analysis show little. It might be argued that if one is liberal one would be led to adopt the feminist position on this measure. It is not possible to separate the effects of liberalism on privatization from the reverse effects, but it is possible to show that the structural variables have different impacts on the two ideologies and hence, to assure the skeptical that there is at least some portion of the variance explained by privatization working in the proposed direction. Analysis of the effects of education and women's roles on both conservatism and privatization shows that employment and education bear the strongest relationship to privatization while

Table 7:4
Determinants of Conservatism and
Privatization, Compared

Determinants	Conservatism	Privatization
Education	-.09	-.21*
Marriage	.13*	.04
Motherhood	-.02	-.06
Homemaking	.08	.19*
R^2	.05	.14
(N)	(515)	(607)

Note. For further explanation see Table 7:3.
*p < .05.

marital status is more related to liberalism (Table 7:4). Thus, we are assured that privatization is not simply a surrogate for liberalism in analysis of political orientations, although they are clearly related. Privatization may be made a liberal-conservative issue but it is also an orientation with sources in women's role structures that are distinct from those of left-right ideology.

Table 7:5
Determinants of Positive Attitude
toward Change in Government

Education	-.02
Marriage	-.10*
Motherhood	.01
Homemaking	.03
Privatization	-.07
R^2	.01
(N)	(509)

Note. For further explanation see Table 7:3.
*p < .05.

What is the nature of the relationship between marriage and conservatism? Some suggestion is provided by our earlier discussion of political trust and protest. Previous research suggests that the norms of ascription, dependence, and removal from outside authorities serves as a basis for some women's faith in authority. These factors, as well as the norm of security and being "settled" may foster conservatism. More evidence is provided by another question asked of the women in this study. Analysis of responses to a question of whether change in our form of government is necessary or not once again shows marriage as a factor (Table 7:5).[23] It appears that marriage as an institution is supportive of conservative norms.

Moralism

Another form of conservatism often thought to be exhibited by women is moralism. A number of psychologists have attempted to analyze sex differences in both moralism and punitiveness. The majority of studies found no differences, some found selective differences.[24] The 1974 Virginia Slims Poll provides some good examples of the types of differences found.[25] The respondents were asked to identify "sufficient reasons for considering divorce." There is only one of thirteen reasons that shows a difference of more than 5 percent between the sexes: 49 percent of the women cite sexual infidelity as opposed to 39 percent of the men. On a related issue, 53 percent of the women and 44 percent of the men felt that premarital sex is immoral.

Many more differences occur on issues relevant to childrearing. Sixty-four percent of the women in the Virginia Slims study would rather err on the side of giving too little freedom (as opposed to too much) to their children in contrast to 54 percent of the men. The respondents were also given a list of activities and asked whether they would "establish strict rules," "set general guidelines," or "let children do as they please." Males and females differed on five of thirteen activities; on each, including "letting you know where they go when they leave the house," "what time they come home at night," "how many nights a week they go out," "the places they go for entertainment," and "how much television they watch," women are more likely than men to establish strict rules. Moreover, 64 percent of the women and 53 percent of the men felt that it is very important for children to get religious training. Other studies show women less favorable toward abortion than are men, but these differences are generally slight.[26]

The question of the relationship between gender roles and moralism is theoretically complex. We might assume that the salience of protection of children is more important to traditionally oriented women than to role transcenders. But can we assume that nontraditional women are not concerned with protection of children and therefore are not as moralistic in their judgments?

A more appealing explanation may be obtained by considering the tradeoffs one must make in taking issue positions. If we design a continuum with moralism at one end, must the other end be immoralism or, in the mind of the individual, is it really something else? We may assume that few of our respondents would claim to support immoralism. They might, however, reject opinions one might accept on the underlying basis of moralism because of another underlying principle, for instance, liberty. The case of pornography is a good example. We might reject the right of a publisher to print pornographic material because we wish to protect the morals of a community. On the other hand, we might support the publisher's right to publish, not solely on the basis of the judgment that pornography is not harmful (or, perhaps, that it is beneficial) to the community, but because we see the potential sacrifice of freedom of speech as greater than the potential sacrifice of moral protection.[27]

If we are to understand public opinion, even on very specific issues, the underlying value tradeoffs must be understood. In the present case of investigation of gender roles the specific issue attitude is only one part of the question. The more compelling point concerns the value preferences linked to a gender role. Hence the analysis presented here tests the relationship between gender roles and moralistic orientation rather than between roles and specific issues.

A number of items in the interview schedule appeared to involve questions of morality, but only two were intercorrelated highly enough to justify combination into an additive index of moralism. The first question is, "Some people think that the use of marijuana should be made legal. Others think that penalties for using marijuana should be set higher than they are now. Where would you place yourself on this scale (1-7)?" The second question is "Some people think it is all right for the public schools to start each day with a prayer. Others feel that religion does not belong in the public schools but should be taken care of by the family and church. Which do you think?" The correlation between these two items is .31 (Pearson r, $p < .01$). Both of these questions involve a tradeoff between morality and rights. It should be noted that although *either* position on these questions, especially on the question of having children pray in public schools, may be considered moral in some sense, moralism is defined here as the protection of traditional morals. Over one third (35 percent) of the women scored high on moralism (penalties should be set higher for marijuana use, prayer should be allowed in school) and 13 percent scored low (marijuana should be legal, no prayer in school).

Liberalism is included in the analysis of moralism in order to distinguish between the effects of privatization as a liberal issue position and privatization as role ideology. Both maternal status and privatization have significant effects on moralism which are independent of both education and liberal-conservative ideology (Table 7:6). There is a tendency for traditionally oriented women and mothers to be more moralistic in their issue stances.

Table 7:6
Determinants of Moralism

Determinants	
Education	$-.17^*$
Marriage	.00
Motherhood	$.14^*$
Homemaking	.03
Conservatism	$.29^*$
Privatization	$.18^*$
R^2	.27
(N)	(438)

Note. For further explanation see Table 7:3.
$^*p < .05$.

Another related issue is tolerance of communists. The women were asked to agree or disagree with the following statement: "If a Communist were legally elected to some public office around here, the people should allow him to take office." This question, of course, concerns the democratic rights of free elections and perhaps some conception of national security. In this country, however, communism is often attributed with immorality, particularly in sexual matters. The nineteenth-century communal movements, which often contained a large element of feminism, were often attacked on these grounds. From the turn of the century, feminism was attacked as both "communist" (originally "bolshevist") and sexually immoral. Red-scare polemics almost invariably include references to "Godless Communism." Regardless of the doctrinaire Marxist rejection of promiscuity as bourgeois decadence, domestic communism is often seen as a moral issue.

In 1955 Samuel Stouffer found that women were less likely than men to allow civil liberties to socialists and communists.[28] He, too, saw the issue as one of moralism, due especially to the churchgoing habits of women. The same is true in this study: 79 percent of the college-educated men and 61 percent of the college-educated women, 50 percent of the male high school graduates and 23 percent of the female high school graduates would allow a communist to take office. These are some of the largest sex differences that appear in these data. Traditionally oriented women, then, should be less willing than the other women to grant civil liberties to communists. In fact, among the high school graduates, 20 percent of the traditionals and 42 percent of the egalitarians feel that a legally elected communist should be allowed to take office. The same is true of 25 percent of the mothers and 41 percent of the nonmothers. College-educated women are more favorable toward granting civil liberties to communists: 31 percent of the traditionals and 71 percent of the feminists support such civil liberties as do 51 percent of the mothers and 67 percent of the nonmothers.

This is the only issue included in this chapter in which it is possible to judge the effects of gender roles and role ideology through use of panel analysis (Table 7:7). Tolerance of communism is related to gender roles in much the same way as is moralism. Mothers are not as favorable toward extending civil liberties to communists as are women without children. Although privatization is related to tolerance of communism, considering it along with maternal status reveals a lack of significant direct effects. It appears that the women evaluate the issues on grounds other than the basic ideological intent of communism. Half the women (49 percent) think an elected communist should be allowed to take office; the responses do not distinguish between those who advocate communism, or even feel sympathetic toward it, and those who do not. Rather, evaluation of the issue is made on the basis of other underlying values of civil liberties or moralism.[29]

Table 7:7
Determinants of Tolerance of Communists

Determinants	Degree of Tolerance (%)
1965 Tolerance	.23
Education	.18*
Marriage	−.03
Motherhood	−.11*
Homemaking	.01
Conservatism	−.17*
Privatization	−.08
R^2	.22
(N)	(501)

Note. For further explanation see Table 7:3.
*$p < .05$.

Why is motherhood in particular associated with conservative stances in politics? Mothers, as pointed out earlier, are responsible for transmitting moral values on a day-to-day basis. Cultural moral values become their responsibility when they have children, and through this responsibility they become agents in their own socialization. The constant maternal exhortations of, "Watch your language," "What do you say?" "Play nicely now," and "Did you write your grandmother?" constitute portions of the daily training in moral values mothers give. How many times do we see young parents begin to enforce moral values on themselves as a result of parenthood? Young parents can be seen cleaning up their own language as their children become old enough to imitate it, joining religious institutions they had abandoned when they left their parents' home, explaining the responsibilities of sexuality they might not have had as adolescents and young adults, and remembering always to say please and thank you in front of their four-year-olds. We might argue that parents, and especially mothers, teach not only their children traditional moral values, but themselves as well.

Nurturance and Care for the Downtrodden: Social Welfare and Racial Equalization

Women have long been noted for engaging in liberal and reform causes. Many of the most well known American women — the suffra-

gists, Sojourner Truth, Dorothea Dix, Jane Addams—were cele-
brated for their reformism. Women's organizations, even including
the Daughters of the American Revolution in its earlier years, were
at the forefront of change and progressivism in the late nineteenth
and early twentieth centuries. Indeed, male Progressives were
attacked by Democrats and Republicans alike for being more like
women than men in their political goals and methods.[30] Leading
feminists usually have been associated with other liberal or leftist
causes.

These liberal causes have generally revolved around the themes
of social welfare and nurturance, both of which can be seen as
extrapolations of domestic values and roles. Documents and speeches
left by earlier female reformers are liberally salted with references
to the effects of the lack of parks, the penal or medical systems,
bossism, or a particular candidate on the home. Even today many
people continue to argue that if women were to occupy more positions of power, governments would be more responsive to social
welfare needs.

Not only well-known female activists are known for their social
welfare attitudes. Women in general are thought to be more social
welfare oriented than are men. The values of nurturance and motherhood have led people to expect women to be especially sensitive
to the needs of the poor and oppressed. Some observers have not
been as generous in their assessment of women and social welfare;
Robert Lane, for one, suggests that the same moralism that leads
women to be conservative motivates them to become involved in
reformism through a "bloodless love of the good."[31] This characterization aside, it is not possible to assume that traditionally
oriented women are more favorable toward social welfare or social
levelling than are egalitarians or less traditionally oriented women.
These positions are, after all, liberal stances, which should be associated with the more progressively thinking women.

One question in this survey tapped attitudes toward social welfare programs that are not specifically oriented toward minority
groups. This question asked respondents to indicate which statement more closely represented their opinions: (1) "The government
in Washington should see to it that every person has a job and a
good standard of living," or (2) "the government should just let each
person get ahead on his own." If women's roles or role ideology

help shape social welfare attitudes, it does not show up here; none of the role variables were significantly related to responses to these statements.

Women's social welfare attitudes are thought to be based not simply in a general tendency toward nurturance, but also in particular sympathy for the weak, poor, or oppressed. Three questions in this survey asked about government intervention in improving the status of minorities. Two concern integration in schools:

> Some people say that the government in Washington should see to it that white and black children are allowed to go to the same schools. Others claim that this is not the government's business. Do you think that the government in Washington should see to it that white and black children go to the same school or stay out of this area as it is none of its business?

> Some people think that achieving racial integration of the school is so important that it justifies busing children to schools out of their neighborhoods. Others think letting children go to their neighborhood schools is so important that they oppose busing. Where would you place yourself on this scale (1-7)?

One is more broadly socio-economic:

> Some people feel that the government in Washington should make every possible effort to improve the social and economic position of blacks and other minority groups. Others feel that the government should not make any special effort to help minorities because they should help themselves. Where would you place yourself on this scale (1-7)?

These items were combined into a simple additive scale measuring the degree to which one is favorable toward government intervention in equalizing the races.[32] Once again education, maternal status, left-right ideology, and privatization should be the relevant determining factors.

The women who scored high on privatization were slightly more opposed to government intervention in racial integration than were the others (Table 7:8). High school graduates were less favorable than college-educated women. Among the high school graduates, 28 percent of the egalitarians and 54 percent of the traditionals were opposed to government intervention. Among the college-educated, 20 percent of the college-educated egalitarians and 42 percent of the traditionals were opposed. Maternal status also bears a direct relationship to attitudes toward governmental intervention in equalization, but not as traditional hypotheses would lead us to believe. Mothers are *less* favorable toward these equalization policies than are childless women.

Table 7:8
Determinants of Favorable Attitudes
toward Government Intervention in
Racial Equalization (Whites Only)

Determinants	
Education	.17*
Marriage	−.05
Motherhood	−.13*
Homemaking	.09
Conservatism	−.35*
Privatization	−.12*
R^2	.25
(N)	(412)

Note. For further explanation see Table 7:3.
*$p < .05$.

Once again it is necessary to consider the findings in terms of value tradeoffs. It might be tempting to say simply that one group is favorable toward racial equality and the other is not, but this explanation would not go far in illuminating political effects of role variations. Rather, it is likely that mothers are less favorable toward governmental intervention in racial matters because of fear for their children. Two of the three items in the racial equalization measure concern school integration, the third can include school integration as well as other matters affecting children. The mothers probably evaluate the racial issue in large part on the basis of their perception of increased potential for problems in their children's schools, while the childless women are "freer" to evaluate the issue on the merits of governmental action in the domain of equality. The distinction is a fine one, but it shows a link between a woman's private role composition and her view of the political world and problems within it.

In summary, any particular sympathy women might have toward government intervention in the social welfare of minority groups does not appear to be derived from their status as mothers, nor is it tied to any traditional role orientation. Egalitarians, that is, women who are relatively sensitive to inequities between the sexes, are slightly more apt to favor government activity in the domain of social welfare. This analysis does not, of course, tap a wide range of issues, and there could be a fairly large amount of variation from one to another. The evidence does suggest, however, that there is a weak relationship between gender role ideology and interventionist orientation, and that the traditionally oriented women take a more laissez-faire stand on these issues.

Party Identification

Most of the references to women's apparent conservatism are based on studies of party identification. We will therefore conclude this analysis of women's points of view with a look at partisanship. We now know that the early studies are seriously out-of-date. In 1968, 1972, 1976, and 1980, American women were slightly more likely to be self-identified Democrats than were men (and less likely to be Independents). In the elections since 1952, women voted in slightly greater proportions for Johnson, Humphrey, McGovern, and Carter in 1980 than did men, although the differences are matters of a few percentage points in either case.[33]

There is little reason to believe that women's adult gender roles per se have direct effects on partisanship. In fact, the women in this study differed in their identification very little in marital, maternal, or employment status, as we should expect. Marital and employment status may, however, serve as mediators in determining what factors do account for women's party identification. Partisanship is learned. Although patterns of partisan identity are often developed during childhood,[34] much may be left to adult socialization. Patterns established in childhood may either be reinforced or broken by the influence of both political events and "significant others" in adulthood. Moreover, with the increase in the number of self-reported Independents, especially among the young, it is possible for spouse or friends to be quite influential in establishing new ties of partisan identity.

The women in the survey were asked to report not only on their own party identification, but also to name the partisan preferences of their mothers, fathers, spouses where applicable, and "most of your friends." Table 7:9 shows the degree to which the women's party identification can be predicted from that of their parents, spouses, and friends.[35] The differences in the proportion of variance explained is impressive; housewives' party identification is quite well accounted for by the identification of their "significant others." The partisan preferences of married women who are employed is less well predicted by others' preferences, and that of single women seems least related to the identification of others. Among married women, those who are employed are more independent of their husbands' views than are homemakers, and the women's mothers' identification is more important for employed women than for homemakers. Finally, the absence of a husband appears to increase the effects of adult peers.

Table 7:9
Impact of "Significant Others' " Partisanship on Self-Reported Partisanship, by Marital and Employment Status

Agreement With	Housewife	Married Employed	Single Employed
Mother	.06	.35*	.43*
Father	.21*	.11*	.17*
Spouse	.67*	.38*	inap
Friends	.02	.05	.21*
R^2	.60	.41	.39
(N)	(106)	(160)	(121)

Note. For further explanation see Table 7:3.
*$p < .05$.

Women's roles and status have increasingly become subjects for discussion within the major political parties beginning, particularly, with the passage of the McGovern-Fraser rules in the Democratic Party and subsequent discussion within both parties in 1972. Although it took until the 1980 election for the two parties to distinguish themselves quite clearly in their attitudes toward women's roles and opportunities, Table 7:10 shows that women who believe that women's place is in the home feel more affinity with the Republican Party than do other women, and women who reject that idea feel closer to the Democrats. Indeed, if we look at identifiers and Independents who lean toward partisanship together, those high on privatization appear equally split in their identification, while those scoring low show a clear preference for the Democratic Party.

Table 7:10
Party Identification, by Privatization

	Privatization		
Party	Low	Medium	High
Identification	(%)	(%)	(%)
Democrat	42	37	33
Ind. (lean Dem.)	17	14	9
Independent	14	16	18
Ind. (lean Rep.)	9	11	13
Republican	19	22	28
Total	101[a]	100	101[a]
(N)	(319)	(247)	(91)

[a]Column does not add to 100% because of rounding error.

We cannot argue that large numbers of women based their partisan identification on their attitudes toward women's roles, but it is possible that their attitudes toward women's roles helps affect the relationship between partisanship and voting behavior. At the time this survey was taken, women's roles had become an issue in presidential politics although not to the degree they did eight years later in the contest among Jimmy Carter, Ronald Reagan, and John Anderson. George McGovern and Richard Nixon represented different stands on issues concerning the status of women; the differences were reflected both in the stands they took and in the very rules and composition of the conventions that nominated them. Once again, although we cannot argue that women's role ideology was responsible for their voting patterns, Table 7:11 reveals an association between the two. The election was characterized by low voter turnout and heavy Democratic defections, resulting in a clear Republican victory. The Democratic women, therefore, pose the most interesting case for analysis. Egalitarian Democrats cast the highest proportion of votes for the Democratic candidate, both because they had the lowest defection rate and because they were relatively likely to vote in the first place. The slightly less egalitarian Democrats were considerably more likely to defect to Nixon, although they voted in substantial (for that election) numbers. The home-oriented women, perhaps the most cross-pressured, show a moderate tendency to defect, but a high tendency to abstain.

In the case of Independents, traditionalists showed a clear pref-

Table 7:11
1972 Presidential Vote, by Party Identification and Privatization

	Privatization								
	Democrats			Independents			Republicans		
Voted For	High (%)	Med. (%)	Low (%)	High (%)	Med. (%)	Low (%)	High (%)	Med. (%)	Low (%)
McGovern	39	43	61	15	18	30	0	4	0
Nixon	25	36	17	56	46	37	82	78	89
Other	4	1	2	3	0	1	0	0	0
No Vote	32	20	20	26	36	32	18	18	11
Total	100	100	100	100	100	100	100	100	100

erence for Nixon, while egalitarians expressed only slightly more support for the winning candidate. Republicans differed very little by role ideology in their presidential votes; the vast majority cast their ballots for the Republican candidate. Gender ideology has rarely played any significant role in the substance of electoral politics. As the election of 1980 further showed, three conditions seem to be necessary for this to occur. First, women's status, and issues concerning women's status, must occupy a major position in the set of issues discussed in a campaign. Second, the candidates must represent themselves very differently with regard to these issues. Third, it must be one in which party defection is common.

Neither party identification nor partisan vote provides evidence that women's traditional roles or role ideology play major roles in leading them toward conservatism. Women's gender ideology may make some differences in their tendency to support one candidate over another, but the likelihood that this serves as the basis of judgment for a large proportion of women is relatively small.

Conclusion

Women are no more of one mind than are men. As most public opinion polls show, the long-held view that women and men have different ways of approaching problems of politics and public policy is simply a commonly held stereotype. Stereotypes, however, are never without any basis in "reality." The analysis presented here suggests what the basis of the mythical "woman's point of view" is.

Socialization and the roles women perform privatize women. As we have argued throughout, "privatization" means not that women perform only private roles, but that these are traditionally seen as the center and focus of women's lives. This is not a "natural" phenomenon; law, policy, and customary division of gender roles help both sexes define the significance of their roles and activities. The point is very simple. The most central aspects of our lives help define the significance of the rest. It is a common observation that lawyers seem to see the legal significance of everything, doctors see the medical significance, artists see the aesthetic significance and — many of us have received this charge — women's studies scholars see the sexist significance. For those women whose central roles concern their families, we would expect to see similar effects.

Although there is not a single women's point of view, women's private roles do help shape their orientations toward political problems. Marriage is associated with conservatism in the sense of rejection of change. Mothers appear more moralistic in their approaches to policy problems, and they were more likely to reject government intervention in racial equalization, particularly where it concerned schools. Privatization was positively associated with favorable attitudes toward government intervention in racial equalization. Democrats were more egalitarian than were Republicans, and egalitarian Democrats were less likely to reject McGovern in 1972 than were the more traditionally oriented women.

Although women's adult roles do help shape women's political values and attitudes, the effects are not as large as some people seem to expect and they certainly do not create what we might call a "woman's point of view." Indeed we should expect other factors such as childhood socialization (especially in the case of party identification), class, and employment to have considerably greater explanatory power. Moreover, we have investigated only a small number of the types of values and attitudes that bear examining. Within the domain of social welfare attitudes, we have no opportunity here to investigate a full range of problems including, for example, education and health. We also have no opportunity to examine the issues raised in the 1970s by the feminist movement. With regard to foreign policy and militarism, although women's roles are supposed to lead them toward particular opposition to war, analysis not displayed here reveals no significant direct effects on attitudes toward the military, the war in Vietnam, or isolationism.

This chapter has looked only at the effects of women's roles on their values and attitudes, not on the salience of particular issues or at their competence in understanding or making decisions about these issues. Until further research is done we might only be able to conclude that women's adult gender roles are linked to political values in complex ways, but that the greater power of the notion of women's unique points of view in politics lies at this time in public stereotypes about their existence.

NOTES

1. Dorothy Sayres, *Are Women Human?* (Grand Rapids: William B. Eerdmans, 1971), pp. 30-31.
2 See David Morgan, *Suffragists and Democrats: The Politics of Woman Suffrage in America* (Ann Arbor: University of Michigan Press, 1972); Virginia Sapiro, "You Can Lead A Lady To The Vote, But What Will She Do With It?" in D. McGuigan, ed., *New Research on Women and Sex Roles* (Ann Arbor: CEW, 1976), pp. 221-37.
3. Maurice Duverger, *The Political Role of Women* (Paris: UNESCO, 1955).
4. Angus Campbell, Philip E. Converse, Warren E. Miller, and Donald E. Stokes, *The American Voter* (New York: Wiley, 1964).
5. Robert Lane, *Political Life* (New York: Free Press, 1959), p. 209.
6. *Ibid.*, pp. 212-13.
7. *Ibid.*, p. 213.
8. Samuel Stouffer, *Communism, Conformity, and Civil Liberties* (New York: Wiley, 1955).
9. Computed from code book marginal frequencies. Louis Harris and Associates, Inc., *The 1972 Virginia Slims American Woman's Poll* (Ann Arbor: ICPSR, 1975). Further information on the study design is available in the codebook.
10. I use the word "stereotypes" advisedly. These beliefs are, by and large, untested generalizations about women as a group that are applied to women as individuals.
11. Talcott Parsons et al., *Family, Socialization and Interaction Process* (Glencoe: Free Press, 1954).
12. Jane Addams, *Newer Ideals of Peace* (Chatauqua, N.Y.: Chatauqua Press, 1907).
13. Aileen Kraditor, *Up From the Pedestal* (Chicago: Quadrangle, 1968), pp. 202-3.
14. For discussions of the argument over a national day care system, see Margaret O'Brien Steinfels, *Who's Minding the Children? The History and Politics of Day Care in America* (New York: Simon and Schuster, 1973).

15. Men provide precious little assistance in childcare, even if their wives have full time jobs. See Kathryn E. Walker, "Time Used by Husbands for Household Work," *Family Economics Review* (June, 1970), 8-11; Shirley S. Angrist, Judith R. Lave, and Richard Mickelsen, "How Working Mothers Manage: Socioeconomic Differences in Work, Child Care, and Household Tasks," *Social Science Quarterly* 56 (Mar., 1976), 641-37; Philip Stone, "Childcare in Twelve Countries," in Alexander Szalai, ed., *The Use of Time* (The Hague: Mouton Publishers, 1972), pp. 249-64.

16. Lane, *Political Life,* p. 213.

17. See especially Roberta S. Sigel and Marilyn Brookes Hoskin, "Perspectives on Adult Political Socialization — Areas of Research," in Stanley Renshon, ed., *Handbook of Political Socialization* (New York: Macmillan, 1977), pp. 259-93.

18. For more discussion, see Holter, *Sex Roles and Social Structure,* pp. 225-31.

19. *Muller* v. *Oregon,* U.S. Supreme Court, 1908.

20. Harriet Holter, *Sex Roles and Social Structure* (Oslo: Universitetsforlaget, 1970).

21. "We hear a lot of talk these days about liberals and conservatives. I'm going to show you a seven-point scale on which the political views that people might hold are arranged from extremely liberal to extremely conservative. Where would you place yourself on this scale, or haven't you thought much about this?"

22. Most of the issue questions were not included in the 1964 wave of the study. Panel analysis is therefore impossible.

23. "Some people believe that a change in our whole form of government is needed to solve the problems facing our country, while others feel no real change is necessary. Where would you place yourself on this scale . . . ? (1-7)"

24. Eleanor Maccoby and Carol Jacklin, *The Psychology of Sex Differences* (Stanford: Stanford University Press, 1974).

25. Roper Organization, *The 1974 Virginia Slims Poll* (New York: 1974).

26. Connie DeBoer, "The Polls: Abortion," *Public Opinion Quarterly* 41 (Winter, 1977-78), 553-64.

27. Or, as is increasingly the case, one might reject the "pornographic right" on the grounds that it represents and condones violence against a particular group of people — women.

28. Stouffer, *Communism, Conformity, and Civil Liberties.*

29. In separate analysis the moralism measure used earlier was found to be significantly related to this question without reducing the explanatory power of motherhood.

30. Robert Marcus, *Grand Old Party: Political Structure in the Gilded Age, 1880-1896* (New York: Oxford, 1971); John Sproat, *The Best Men: Liberal Reformers in the Gilded Age* (New York: 1968).

31. Lane, *Political Life,* p. 212.

32. The latter two items were trichotomized (1-2, 3-5, 6-7) and the items
    were summed. The intercorrelations are (all p < .01):

Gov't Help	1.00		
Bus.	.33	1.00	
Integr.	.32	.35	1.00
	Gov't	Bus.	Integr.

    Only Whites are included in this analysis. Unfortunately the number
    of black women in the sample did not allow separate analysis.
33. Naomi Lynn, "American Women and the Political Process," in J. Free-
    man, ed., *Women: A Feminist Perspective* (Palo Alto: Mayfield, 1979),
    pp. 404-29.
34. M. Kent Jennings and Richard G. Niemi, *The Political Character of
    Adolescence* (Princeton: Princeton University Press, 1974).
35. Partisan identification is constructed in the following standard form.
    Respondents were asked, "Generally speaking, do you usually think
    of yourself as a Republican, a Democrat, an Independent, or what?"
    If the respondent said she was an Independent, she was then asked,
    "Do you think of yourself as closer to the Republican or to the
    Democratic Party?" The resulting code is (1) Democrats: those who
    said they were Democrats, (2) Independents (lean Democrat): those
    who said they were Independents but felt closer to the Democrats,
    (3) Independents: those who said they were Independents and said
    they didn't feel closer to either party, (4) Independents (lean Repub-
    lican): those who said they were Independent but felt closer to the
    Republicans, and (5) Republicans: those who said they were Republi-
    cans. The respondents were asked similar questions about their parents
    and spouses. For purposes of analyzing the relationship between the
    respondents' partisanship and that of "significant others," partisanship
    was simply categorized as Democratic, Independent, and Republican.
    In the case of friends' partisanship respondents were asked, "Are most
    of your friends Republicans or Democrats, or aren't you sure what
    they are?" If they weren't sure they were asked to guess. The variable
    is coded: (1) Democratic: those who said or guessed Democratic, (2)
    Independent/Mixed: those who said or guessed either Independent or
    "half and half," and (3) Republican: those who said or guessed Repub-
    lican.
    It should be noted that a person's perception even of his or her
    spouse's partisan identification is not necessarily correct. For a very
    interesting discussion, based on the 1965 wave of the survey used here,
    see Richard G. Niemi, *How Family Members Perceive Each Other*
    (New Haven: Yale University Press, 1974), especially Chapter VII.

CHAPTER 8

Political Integration
and Social Policy: The Personal
as Political

We have examined the lives of women whom we would expect to have cast off the veils that have enshrouded women in the past. These are young women, women who have had only a few years' experience in adult roles and institutions. They grew up during a time of great social change and attention to questions of expansion of rights and liberties. They are well educated; all of them finished high school and about half went to college. They were of college age during the years of the antiwar movement, the Woodstock celebration and the counterculture, the May Revolt in Paris, the horrors of the 1968 presidential nominating conventions and campaign session, black separatism, and the dawning of the Women's Liberation Movement. These are members of the first generation of "new women."

These "new women" are not fully integrated into the political system at the mass level. They are still embedded in a gender-differentiated social structure. Most of them do not believe fully in the equality of women and men; rather, they accept the traditional ideology of privatization at least in part. There is no reason to have believed that these women would have demonstrated any more radical egalitarianism. Even at the date of this writing and, one suspects, some years hence, the world remains uncomfortable for those who fully believe in the equality of women and men.

Each aspect of women's private roles we have investigated — marriage, motherhood, homemaking, and the underlying ideology of privatization — has political significance and consequences. Where we find that traditional women's roles have some bearing on their political orientations or behavior, we find the effect is to foster the political marginality of women, to impede their integration into politics.

There is little doubt that change is occurring. Women are becoming involved in all aspects of social life, including politics. Women are becoming more responsible for their lives and are making more conscious choices. As for the changes that remain to be made, the "passing fad" of feminist activism is now over a decade old and it continues to grow. But increasing integration of women into politics is not inevitable, it will result only through determined efforts to change. Some of these efforts will involve changes in social policy, many of these changes do not appear at first glance to have direct consequences for women's roles as citizens. Our analysis of the linkages between private and political roles offers a number of clues to the nature of the changes that would be required were America to become favorable toward a full citizenship for women.

Political Opportunity and Integration

We began by discussing the relationship between rights and political integration (Chapter 2). Women were actively involved in politics before many rights of citizenship were granted to them. The granting of explicitly political rights did not signal the completion of women's integration into the political system, even at the mass level. Guarantees of explicitly political rights such as the franchise represent only one stage in the opening up of opportunities.

The basic rights to vote or hold office open up opportunities that may be accepted or rejected. One needs a certain level of resources in order to take advantage of those opportunities. Included among these resources are time and energy, knowledge, interest, a sense of self-worth, and a sense that action is possible, appropriate, and worthwhile. Any policies that restrict a group's access to these resources also limit their political rights. As Sidney Verba, Noman Nie, and Jae-on Kim wrote: "A policy that limited the amount of political knowledge a citizen could acquire or that restricted the right to be as convincing and articulate as possible in expressing his or her preferences to a political leader would hardly be consistent with democratic rights."[1] A full right to citizenship is directly bound up with other social policies that, at first glance, might appear removed from the basic question of political opportunity. For evidence of governmental support and guarantees of political integration we would have to look well beyond the Nineteenth Amendment to the Constitution.

Let us take Verba, Nie, and Kim's example as an illustration. Knowledge and the ability "to be as convincing and articulate as possible" are exactly the kind of resources to which women have had limited access. Through the influence of the various agents of socialization, women are diverted away from knowledge and expertise in many important areas, including politics. Studies of language development show that females are "better" than males and at a younger age; that is, they excel in language skills including the use of grammar. But as we have seen (Chapter 6), studies of language development also show that the style of female language, although more likely to be grammatically correct, is less convincing. As long as the learning of dominance behavior teaches men habitually to interrupt women and demand the lead in conversation, women will appear to be less articulate. Women's language is unconvincing to men because men refuse to be convinced by anyone other than another man. Women's language is the language of the noninfluential, of those who are deferential and dependent. As we have seen, women's roles in the family and the ideology of privatization they continue to learn restrict specifically political knowledge and the ability to communicate, especially in an effort to influence.

Just as women's roles may restrict the resources women need to be integrated into politics as full citizens, so may women's participation in "female" roles in the family and workplace teach them to be something other than full citizens. Women may learn not to use the resources they do have for citizenship. In Chapter 5 we discussed three different approaches to understanding the value of participation, including the idea of civic education. Carole Pateman's book, *Participation and Democratic Theory*, represents an attempt to reinstate the idea of participation as the core of democratic theory.[2] She discusses participation not as ritualistic symbols of membership in the community or even as a mechanism provided for the defense of one's interest. Rather, she points to participation as a constant education in autonomy and self-control (the development of political efficacy) and in public spiritedness, which must include a sense of justice. The primary goals of democratic participation, she argues, are "the development of politically relevant and necessary qualities in the ordinary individual,"[3] the "production of an educated, active citizenry."[4]

Pateman's study of industrial democracy is consistent with other studies that might suggest that democratic roles in explicitly political institutions are not sufficient for reaching these goals.[5] If the norms and rules of other important institutions are at odds with those of the political system, one's "democratic education" is incomplete at best, contradictory at worst. If we push further and ask from what institution will the impact of political education be the greatest, we may, with strong reason, suggest that the institutions which are most salient to individuals' day-to-day lives, and those in which they spend the most time are the most powerful agents of adult socialization. This response turns our attention back to two agents: the family and the workplace. Of course in discussing women and politics, the family and the workplace are one and the same institution for a large proportion of women.

We have argued that participation — not just in politics, but other aspects of social life as well — must be seen as central to any consideration of democratic theory, in part because of the educational function of participation. Thus we may also argue that socialization, and by this we mean socialization over the entire lifespan, must also be regarded as an important component of democratic theory. Chapter 3 argued that we lose much explanatory power by focusing solely on childhood socialization in an effort to determine how individuals become integrated in cultural systems. Rather, individuals' adult work and family roles continue the process of political socialization. It may be jarring to the ears of students of socialization to label one's own social roles as socialization agents. We generally think of agents as others. Indeed, we are suggesting that in adulthood one of the major socialization agents is the individual herself or himself. Norms of responsibility, as Chapter 3 argued, lead us to adopt values and behavior, for example with respect to our parental roles, that have repercussions to other parts of our social life including, as we have seen, politics. Despite the chaos we witness within the family now, that institution is, for adults, perhaps the primary brake on change in systems of gender stratification. The family may not be a stabilizing influence, particularly as familial and public norms begin to diverge, but it will be a conservatizing influence.

To draw our argument full circle, if social policies support institutional structures and pressures that limit women's access to resources necessary for political integration, if they help make the norms of women's private lives inconsistent with those of a political life, or if policies are rejected that would leave women freer to participate in the governance of their own lives through the political system, those policymaking agencies are impeding women's opportunities to take the opportunities "guaranteed" by statements of political rights. We have seen that women's integration into politics is in part contingent upon the private roles they adopt; those who conform to traditional conceptions of women's roles are more marginal to politics than are those who don't. How does social policy limit the choices and opportunities of women? What follows is a review of the findings of this study, set in the context of relevant social policy problems.

The Political Economy of Family and Work

As discussed earlier, if we want to understand the relevance of gender in women's political lives, we cannot talk about a single role (Chapter 4). Even with the stereotype of what women are supposed to do, there are at least three interrelated but distinct roles women perform in the family: wife, mother, and homemaker. These roles involve different activities and somewhat different norms. Most women are probably surprised when they find these three roles can come into mutual conflict in a variety of situations. These roles also bear different relationships to different aspects of political life. An assessment of each follows.[6]

MARRIAGE

The women who were married were less favorable toward the women's movement, more trusting in political leaders, less likely to participate in protest activities, more conservative, and less favorable toward change in government than were women who were not married. The institution of marriage appears bound up with security, faith in authority, and a rejection of change in authority relations. Marital status also promoted or constrained the effects of other roles, education, and earlier political predispositions on political roles. In many cases, marriage appeared to reduce the effects of predispositions found in 1965; it therefore appears to represent a radical juncture in women's lives. Although it is true that much of girls' childhood socialization is devoted to preparation for marriage, marriage itself plays a role in shaping women's political lives.

Marriage and attitudes toward stability and authority appear to be linked in a number of ways. First, as our discussion of socialization (Chapter 3) suggests, getting married is a sign of adulthood, of responsibility for enacting the norms one has been taught. If one chooses to live another way as an adult, she (or he) is often interpreted expressly as "questioning authority" or "rebelling." Once married, a couple is expected to stay that way in the face of all odds. The problem here is not necessarily the social dictum that marriages are not to be taken lightly, but rather the reasons that are offered, in effect, the definition of "responsibility." An excellent example of the implications of "responsibility" is suggested by a 1979 article in one of the most popular magazines, *Newsweek*, in which Suzanne Britt Jordan offered a defense of the "marriage fortress."[7] Her objection was to "the flippancy with which we may say goodbye to a mediocre or poor marriage." "Marriage is nothing more nor less than a permanent promise between two consenting adults, and often, but not always, under God, to cling to each other unto death." She argued that just as one cannot deny kinship to one's blood relatives, "the husband and wife are one flesh, forever." Jordan poses interesting responses to two common reasons for divorce. To the problem of a stifling marriage that appears to deny personal growth and autonomy she objects, "As for finding myself, I think I already know who I am, *I'm grown up; I have responsibilities; I am in the middle of a lifelong marriage* . . . ." To the problem of "marriages that defy hell itself" she writes, "Spouses may be psychotic, alcoholic, sexually perverted, or dangerous. Yet, we *do* promise to remain faithful in sickness and in health." To the people who wonder why many of the thousands of women who undergo physical violence and abuse from their husbands stay with their prisonkeepers, Jordan provides an answer.

These passages do not provide examples of great social science or social theory. They do illustrate something of the meaning of marriage to many people. It is a sign of responsibility; it is, as Jordan mentions twice, a duty, and it is an institution that demands respect and faith long after one has lost respect for one's partner, if things come to that. The authoritativeness of the marriage contract is in many ways more important than what goes on in the decades that follow. Women also learn to see marriage as security itself. They learn that in marriage they will be protected, loved, respected, and successful as a woman. Threats to marriage are profound threats to self-identity.

Social custom and law make married women dependent upon the good will of others and on the stability of the marriage. The law defines the husband as the head of the household.[8] This means, first, that in most states his domicile and that of his wife are determined by his residence alone. If he moves to get a better job and she refuses to follow because she would lose a good job, she is deserting him. If she moves to get a better job and he refuses to follow because he would lose a good job, she is also deserting him. Marriage marks consent to sexual relations between husband and wife, therefore in most states there is no such thing as rape in marriage. Once married, a woman must depend on a man's good will in not having sexual relations with her against her will because in most states she has already granted her consent through her marriage vows—she has no will. If a husband beats his wife, which happens more commonly than most people are willing to believe, there is virtually no protection for the wife, unless she lives in one of the few communities in which a woman's organization has established a "safe house," a shelter for battered wives with no public knowledge of the address. In most cases, given the ideology of marriage and gender roles, most people—including law enforcement agencies and the woman herself—believe the woman must have done something to "deserve" the abuse.[9]

In economic matters the husband is supposed to provide support for the wife. Most courts, however, accept the precedent that if a woman continues to live with her husband, that is proof enough that he is supporting her regardless of how much or little support he actually provides. The property laws of forty-two states (common law property) state that marital property belongs to the person who holds title; in the absence of title the breadwinner (male) is generally considered the owner. The result is that wives — especially those who follow social dictates and are homemakers — have few rights to property. The effects of these laws are particularly painful in the case of widowhood. Indeed, in the event of the end of a marriage by death or divorce, women often find themselves worse off than when they started, often with the added burden of dependent children.

For our purposes these laws combine to mean a woman must place faith in the good graces of their husbands, and would have good reason to be fearful of changes that might throw off the delicate balance of their marital relationships. It is common to see ripples of fear run through a community of married people when a couple's marriage fails. We may speculate that what links marriage to a need for security is not that marriage means living permanently in a relattionship that grants security, but rather that marriage means living "permanently" in a relationship where one's security is constantly under threat. Depending on the character of one's husband, security may be based on personal acquiescence and the sheer belief that despite everything, the institution of marriage, in general and specific, must last as long as both partners live.

The character of marriage varies widely, of course; the laws and policies that enforce dependency will have no effect on a couple as long as both parties continue to love each other, the husband and wife treat each other well, the wife is well provided for, there is no threat of divorce, abandonment, or one party dying, and there is no reason to believe that any of these conditions will change. Otherwise, marital law and family policy help maintain acquiescence among women.

MOTHERHOOD

Motherhood has different effects on women's political roles depending on other aspects of their lives. Motherhood has an inhibiting effect on political efficacy and, among married women, on political knowledge. In terms of political participation, the greatest impact of motherhood is on single women. Among single women motherhood restricts the tendency to try to influence other people and the communication networks through which one may influence others, it depresses voting turnout and campaign activity. These results show the major problems women confront when they are left to raise children on their own; considering that by the middle of the 1970s there were 6.6 million female-headed families, we are talking about an important sector of the U.S. population.[10] As divorce rates continue to rise without an equivalent rise in the number of men seeking custody of their children, the number of single mothers will also rise. Can we argue that social policy contributes to the political problems of single mothers?

The first contribution of policy to single motherhood is that government policies regarding fertility control help increase, or at least do little to decrease, the number of pregnancies among women who do not want or cannot care for children. Government is responsible for establishing the basic contours of education. The core curriculum of public education is designed to insure a basically responsible, informed public. Thus, boards of education require basic math and reading skills, civics, education, physical education ("gym"), and many require foreign languages, first aid ("health" education), and even driver education on the principle that basic training in these areas is essential to the ability to function intelligently and responsibly as adults. In contrast, many of these same boards of education assume that basic training in reproductive systems (including pictures) and sexuality is antithetical to being able to function intelligently and responsibly as adults. Many local communities feel that this type of training is best left to parents, many of whom got their training from the next-door adolescent years before.

Other policies in the late 1970s also contribute to unwanted and dangerous pregnancies. Only in 1971 did it become unconstitutional to bar single people from obtaining contraceptive devices,[11] and in 1973 it became unconstitutional to place an outright ban on abortion.[12] Another decision, however, maintained the constitutionality of barring the use of public money to pay for abortions.[13] Regardless of one's view of abortion, one fact cannot be denied: the effect of this ruling is completely to deny access to a safe abortion only to those who can least afford to raise a child. In many states this ruling also means that women must carry the result of incest and rape.

Other policies help promote problems for single mothers. Only recently have some states begun to enforce child support ruling by courts at all vigorously. Studies show that after one year, only about half of the fathers who were ordered by the courts to provide some child support actually do so.[14] As a result, many single mothers must turn to public assistance to help support their children. Here there are problems also. The policies undergirding AFDC and other child support programs are often demoralizing and insulting to the women who seek assistance; the public image of welfare mothers continues to be the undeserving leech seeking a handout. This image stands in sharp contrast to the reality, which is that a large proportion of children who receive AFDC assistance have been abandoned financially by their fathers and have undertrained mothers.[15] Public assistance programs that may help single mothers are also traps. In order to qualify for assistance, a mother must seek employment. If, during her marriage, she had done what was expected of her and was a homemaker, thus having little job experience and perhaps not enough training or education to find a stable, secure job, she is in trouble. Most AFDC programs will not support a child while a mother seeks the education necessary to have a good chance of permanently losing the need to be supported by social welfare money. The cycle of dependence continues.

One of the primary problems of single mothers, other than a lack of financial support, but related to it, is a lack of time and energy. The public sector has taken virtually no responsibility for the care of children whose parents are employed and cannot be present to look after them and especially, who cannot afford the expense of private babysitters and day care centers. Interestingly, there was a time when the public sector did move toward seeing day care as a community responsibility: during World War II when women were encouraged to "take up the slack" and work in war industries.[16] As soon as the war was over, women, ever the marginal force, were urged to "go home" and the government abandoned the idea of public responsibility for children.

Public policy, then, helps to develop an increasing population of single mothers who are left to struggle for themselves. These policies also help to keep these same women as marginal to the political system. They are constrained in their ability to take an active role in the public sector by the same policies that create major economic and social problems for them. When they are given public assistance, it is seen as a "handout" and they are seen as burdens. Not all single mothers are destitute, of course, and not all are single mothers involuntarily. Increasing numbers of single women with the financial means to support a child are choosing to become mothers. Even in these cases there are some severe problems. A child who is born of a mother who is not married is considered "illegitimate," a label with negative legal and social implications for both mother and child. Women continue to be told that they are most fulfilled when they comply with their "maternal instincts" and give birth to a child, but it still appears that these instincts are only "legitimate" among women who accept a man as the head of the household. Most research shows, however, that the man is generally not very involved in care giving.[17] That is her responsibility and — in the face of little assistance — her burden.

Motherhood appears to have different political consequences for women who are married, but only under certain circumstances. Our analysis provides evidence that children may provide women with important links to the political world. Among women who did not go to college, motherhood appears to promote community activism; among homemakers, motherhood is related to interest in politics beyond the local and state level and increases the number of communication networks within which women try to exert influence. For these women, a child appears to serve as a channel through which to see one's connection to politics.

Motherhood is also related to women's approach to political issues and problems. The women with children are more moralistic, less tolerant of civil liberties if they conflict with moralism, and less favorable toward government intervention in racial equalization. This analysis provides evidence that if women seem to have different and more parochial views of political problems than do men as a group, it is not because these are natural to women; it is because of the division of labor and the responsibilities women assume when they become mothers. If women continue to be confined to special social tasks, including the moral training of children, simply because they are women, we may expect this state of affairs to continue. If mothers and fathers were brought up to see both home and public responsibilities as equally theirs, would one sex have a greater tendency toward parochialism? We doubt it.

EMPLOYMENT

One of the ways in which this analysis differs most from prior research on women and politics is the lack of power of employment status in explaining women's political roles. Homemaking is directly associated with privatization, it seemed to constrain the number and types of communication networks through which women exert influence, and it inhibited women's interest in national and international politics. Homemaking, therefore, is partially responsible for the parochialism and privatization observed among women, but its effects on most forms of participation and most orientations and attitudes are indirect. In Chapter 2 we pointed out that in many ways the differences between homemaking as an occupation and other occupations women commonly hold are not that different. Employed women, even highly trained professionals, tend to be concentrated in distinctly "female" sectors of the labor market. Women's jobs tend to be analogous to the roles women perform in the home. Moreover, given the division of labor between husband and wife, father and mother, there is a sense in which most women who have husbands and children are homemakers even if they are employed full time or more outside the home. The employment of women has little to do with the proportion of housework and childcare they do vis à vis their husbands.[18]

In what manner should we expect homemaking to be related to political roles and opportunities? The relationship should depend on women's interpretations of the meaning of their work, and of their time. Thus we find that women who are homemakers but have no children are more parochial than homemakers who have children. We also find that the degree to which homemakers become involved in campaign activities depends upon whether they interpret their roles as privatized or not. Homemakers' level of conceptualization of politics also depends on their degree of privatization. In contrast, employed married women seem more affected by education than are homemakers in their level of political interest, the level of government in which they are interested, their trust in government officials, and turnout. In only one case, the number of communication networks through which women exert influence, were homemakers more affected by education than were employed women. In terms of political integration, the most severe problem homemakers face is the possibility that the walls of the home can become a barricade. This possibility depends very much on policies regarding marriage and motherhood, and on women's interpretations of themselves, or privatization.

One of the most important effects of employment is in changing women's conceptions of their own roles. As prior research shows, women in the labor force are more likely to believe in the equality of women and men than are homemakers. Myra Feree suggests that the direction of causality is from employment status to egalitarianism rather than the reverse.[19] Women who seek employment for financial reasons, as is the case with most, learn new attitudes toward and beliefs about women from their experiences.

PRIVATIZATION

The norm of privatization is most consistently related to the various aspects of political integration we have investigated. Women who accept that notion that women's lives revolve around the home are, of course, less likely to be feminists than are other women, but they also display lower levels of political knowledge, sophistication, and efficacy, they are less interested in national and international politics, they believe in a more supportive, less active form of citizenship, they have fewer communication networks through which they exert influence, they are less likely to participate in protest activities, if they are married they are less likely to write letters to editors on political subjects, and if they are homemakers they are not as active in campaigning as are other women. In addition, privatized women are more conservative and moralistic, and less favorable toward government intervention in racial equalization. Privatized women constitute the picture of traditional femininity. They also constitute the picture of political marginality.

Fewer women than ever regard the home as the only place where they may live, work, and devote their attentions. But, as we argued from the beginning, even when women venture into the public world, the home and the private virtues of femininity may still dominate the way they think about themselves and the way others think about them. When men seek jobs no one asks them, "But who will care for the children?" When men seek jobs few would suggest that they take part-time jobs so they can be available if their children need them. No one suggests that a married man cannot be a good representative in Congress because he will exhibit only parochial concerns for his wife and children. These concerns are addressed to women, however, because no matter what they do in public, their private lives are the measure by which they are evaluated.

Eliminating laws that barred women from public pursuits does not constitute a change sufficient to integrate women into the political system as full citizens. Political femininity, privatization, must be eliminated. Femininity is not a biological fact, it is a state of mind through which one interprets one's connections to others and to social institutions. Elimination of explicitly political barriers to women's citizenship was therefore a first step toward integration. Elimination of the social and economic barriers concerning family and economic policy is the ongoing second step. Elimination of the psychological barriers through a new type of civic education will be the third step.

Civic Education and the Integration of Politics and Personal Life

We have returned to the questions of culture raised in Chapter 2. If women are to become integrated into political life as full citizens, cultural change is necessary. Women cannot simply be invited to join in politics when their childcare schedules allow. The "webs of significance," or assumed givens about women and, as we shall argue, about politics, must change as well. We now turn directly to some prescriptive conclusions.

In the past few centuries we have divided the world into the separate spheres of the public and private. The public sphere, with its set of rules and morality, is where we find government. The private sphere, with its set of rules and morality, is where we find the family and most of women's work. Women are no longer restricted to private activities, but whatever women do they are cloaked in a veil of privatization. It is, as we have argued, more important to know what a woman has "done with" her children than it is to know what a man has done with his. It is more important to know whose wife she is than it is to know whose husband he is. A wife is usually labeled with her husband's name rather than the reverse. When women have rejected the veil of privatization, it remains notable by its absence.

Law and policy have been premised on women's ties to the private sphere. So have education and moral training. In recent years many of the relevant restrictive laws and policies have been altered or abolished. The earliest changes concerned basic property, education, political, and employment rights. In recent years there have been more profound legal changes in these areas. The last policies to change, and those that contain the most damaging restraints, concern the more private aspects of life: marriage, reproduction, childcare, and sexuality.

These changes remove many of the most tangible constraints on women's ability to participate in the life of the community; women are now technically allowed to enter nearly any pursuit they desire. But there is a vast difference between allowing the participation of women on the one hand and including participation and membership as a public value on the other. The distinction is the difference between a policy of toleration and one of liberation. "Toleration" is a long-standing option for a heterogeneous society and one which in many ways is the buttressing principle of the ideology of liberal pluralism. Toleration is not an active principle, it is a passive one. It places a premium on the elimination of tangible barriers but makes no commitment to a positive value of inclusion and membership. To "tolerate" indicates the tolerated idea or person is essentially regarded as deviant. "To tolerate," as the *Oxford English Dictionary* says, means "to endure," "to allow," "to suffer," "to put up with."

A policy of liberation requires placing positive value on membership. It would reduce not simply the tangible barriers to inclusion, but also the psychological and cultural. Political liberation of women, therefore, would mean that women would be seen not as deviants, or even as welcome strangers. Liberation would mean that our very conception of women would be changed from what it is now. As long as women are interpreted as primarily private persons, distinct from, although allowed entry into public matters such as politics, women cannot be fully integrated into the political world. They will continue to be seen as responsible first and foremost for the private activities of the community.

Some strides have been made in the direction of changing the definition of women. Much of the change has taken place because the reality of women's lives has become increasingly inconsistent with the traditional ideology and image. "Woman" and "mother" simply cannot remain pure synonyms as women gain more control over fertility and spend smaller and smaller periods of their lives surrounded by babies. "Woman" and "homemaker" are also losing their senses of interchangeability as a majority of women take their places in the workforce. Each day there are fewer occupations and life pursuits for which one can say women cannot be capable because there are capable women in almost every pursuit, even if in only token numbers. As women go about the business of their day-to-day lives, they will break the "rules" of femininity until, at least in some sectors of society, to argue that women are naturally irrational, submissive, petty, or parochial will be laughable.

Some policies aimed at changing the definition of women are currently being pursued. Women's groups have demanded changes in educational curricula and content, and many educational institutions are beginning to comply. Until more recent policy changes many schools and occupational organizations were beginning to comply with government order that they take "affirmative action" to insure that they were not discriminating against women. These policies, when enforced, stand in stark contrast to the older negative policies of toleration in which organizations had simply to agree not to discriminate actively against women.[20] These changes are not sufficient, however. If the most private relations are not altered, those involving reproduction, sexuality, and the family, women's involvement in politics and economics will simply be an overlay, an added burden to their lives. If private relations are not altered, women will continue to have primary responsibility for the private sphere and their integration into the public will not be complete.

One may well ask who will care for the children if private relations are altered and women become integrated into the public sphere. The question is asked practically and symbolically. On the practical side, the image of the latch-key child has not left us. Many people continue to fear that if women become fully active in the public sphere there will be "no one" to fill the human needs of the private sphere. On the symbolic side the question stands for much more than childcare per se. Many fear that if women become fully integrated into the public sphere they will have to lose the "good" qualities associated with women and femininity including, especially, nurturance. The world, some say, will become a passionless, sterile, and "unisex" (which means boring) place.

These speculations are not totally without substance. Full political integration will require that women not bear nearly sole responsibility for children and home, that women cannot be counted on to take care of all problems when action is not convenient for men. Full integration will also require that women lose a number of characteristics labelled "feminine." Among these are submissiveness, oppressive selflessness, low self-esteem, deference based on ascriptive status, and an unwillingness to recognize themselves as autonomous persons. This does not mean that women will have to lack nurturance, a willingness to give, the ability to laugh and cry, or a capability for sensuality. What will be lost is femininity as it has been idealized, a cultural construct premised on living through other people, especially husbands and children.

But again, we ask, who will care for the children? Who will take responsibility for private needs? This persistent question reveals the extent of change in both the public and private sphere necessary for integration of women into the political world. Asking who will bear responsibility for private matters if women become more integrated into the public world is an indication of the degree to which men are not integrated into the private world. Jean Elshtain has argued that men share in both the public and private spheres, in comparison with women who are ever under the veils of the private.[21] It may be closer to the truth to argue that men are nearly as little integrated into the family as women are integrated into public pursuits. The primary difference — admittedly a crucial one — is that men have tremendous authority in the private sphere as women do not in the public. Men are, however, absentee landlords in many senses, so much so that in contrast to women, having children has relatively little effect on men's sense of identity, their occupations, interests, and, as some evidence shows, their political pursuits.[22]

Men's lack of integration and responsibility in the family is displayed most clearly by men who are faced for the first time with the need to give primary attention to their children as a result of divorce. Divorced fathers often report they never realized how little attention they had given their children or how little sense they had of "what to do" with them during visits. In a sense, these men are faced with learning the difference between babysitting and parenting.[23] Even more revealing are the changes experienced by men who accept joint custody of their children. Men who, for the first time, have primary responsibility for family life for extended periods of time find that their sense of self changes, their relationship with their children is qualitatively different, family responsibilities play a larger role in all facets of their lives, and, as important for our point here, their understanding of and respect for women increases.[24] The public is only dimly aware of these problems. Well over a decade after the women's movement began publicizing the problems of divisions of labor within the family, the Academy-award-winning film, *Kramer* vs. *Kramer* was a shock and an education to many people. But the remaining ideology of female privatization meant that the education still could not be complete. Tremendous audience sympathy is aroused by the months the man spends raising a child by himself. The sympathy raised by his months generally appeared to outweigh the sympathy for her years of performing the same task.

One of the conditions for the integration of women into the public sphere is the integration of men into the private sphere. This change cannot be regarded as a simple matter of having men spend more time and attention on their children. Once again one of the major issues is the significance of human activities, the definitions we attach to them. If men devote more time to domestic life, but if, in performing these tasks, they continue to be defined as "helping their wives," the significance of their activities and the definitions of male and female roles have changed only part way. The changes necessary for political integration would have profound implications for the quality and structure of all aspects of life, including politics. The public world of politics is currently structured by and around men. The institutions, procedures, informal rules, and substantive concerns of political organizations are not natural phenomena, spontaneously springing from the earth, sea, or air. They are and have been designed by men, and designed by men in their own images.[25] What almost all political theorists but the most radically feminist seem to ignore is that these organizations are designed by men who have not had primary responsibility for the day-to-day maintenance of life. The people who are responsible for the method and substance of politics can work free of many of the bonds of human necessity because their children are nurtured by women, and they, themselves are fed by women and clothed by women, and their houses are cleaned by women. Because the people who organize and direct public organizations do not, in a relative sense, have to take private needs and responsibilities into account in their public lives, neither do the rules, procedures, and content of those organizations. This argument does not amount to a conspiracy theory; rather, the point is a social-psychological one.

The radical differentiation of human activity into public and private spheres is generally accepted as a natural part of an efficient, modern life. Increasing numbers of people are noting that this differentiation has gone too far.[26] The private sphere, and women along with it, now appear parochial and even embarrassing because of a lack of connection to public life and values; the public sphere, and men along with it, appear sterile and impoverished because of a lack of connection to private life and values. The modern political community cannot or will not take into account those things that make us fundamentally human. As Robert Paul Wolff has eloquently pointed out, modern political norms of equity, fairness, rights, and rationality, embodied in liberal, especially contract political theories, make the private world, which is populated primarily by women and children, off-bounds to public consideration. In these theories, Wolff writes:

> This systematic setting to one side of the fundamental facts of birth, childhood, parenthood, old age, and death results in an image of the public or political world as a timeless or static community of adults, met together to transact their collective business. Periodically, a citizen dies, or a youngster is certified as adult and admitted to the body politic. But nothing in the theory suggests that there is any significant difference between the birth of a child and the granting of a provisional entrance visa to a foreigner, or between the death of a citizen and his emigration.[27]

Public affairs do not take full account of these events, and the organizations of public life are not designed for the entrance of people who take full account of these events because the people who have run public life have not needed to do so.

We have come to one more sign that political procedures of tolerance of women in politics cannot work. Women will not fit into politics if public affairs remains as it is, functionally and normatively detached from private life. A policy of promotion of women into public affairs will not work if the private world is not integrated.[28] Finally, the public world of politics will not remain the same if its population — regardless of its gender composition — is integrated as well into what is now the private world. If public people know what it is to have direct and personal responsibility for the lives of children, it cannot be so obvious that public funding of a bankrupt manufacturer of bombers is more important than public funding of childcare facilities and fertility control. Only a radically bifurcated society could regard bombers as public goods and children as private goods. Procedures of public organizations will have to take into account the private obligations of individuals.

At this point in the discussion, in which we envision a time of integration of both the public and private spheres, we have arrived at the point of profound cultural change suggested earlier. Now the "people" are not as distinct from the "public." The public and private spheres have lost their distinct meanings as well. We have moved beyond a culture with an odd configuration of values in which people — women-people — care for the children but the public does not, in which the "men" of public affairs care for the public but not the people, in which the most basic human needs are not the central concerns of the community, as expressed by its decision-making processes and organizations.

Pateman, among others, suggests that a major function of democratic participation is a civic education that allows a person to see and act upon the connections between the public and private spheres.[29] The problem with this approach, in the context of current conceptions of individual and community life, is that in fundamental ways public and private life are in conflict with each other. Thus we find that acceptance of private life as it has existed for women bars their integration into politics even at the most basic citizen levels. Civic education of the type Pateman envisions is possible only where coherent connections among the different facets of individual and community existence are there to be learned.

To summarize and conclude, we may ask three final questions. Who will care for the children during a time of political integration? The community will. Women, as private individuals, are already doing their part — more than their part — in nurturing the next generation. They are, wherever is possible, with our current institutional arrangements, giving each other assistance as family, friends, and professionals.[30] Men will have to learn from women how to join in this crucial and humanizing endeavor.[31] Men and women together, as actors in the public community and for the public good, will have to lend support in every way necessary to the raising of the community's new members. Children are not "private goods"; without them we have no future. Therefore the task of childcare is not a purely private matter; it is a public obligation.

As we have seen, motherhood is not the only private role that affects women's lives as citizens; marriage does as well. A second question that might be asked, therefore, is "who will care for the men?" This question is not often asked with the force of the first question, but it may well be as central in the minds of those who object to the loosening of women's apron strings. Males are cared for by their mothers until they are cared for by their wives in general. We even see men who, in the absence of a wife or mother, must depend upon their female children, who may be more competent at day-to-day care than the adult man himself. Marriage often, although not necessarily, leads to a dual dependency that strikes doubly at women, and simultaneously frees and limits them. Women who learn they must depend upon a husband learn a form of love based on self-sacrifice and selfless altruism. They put themselves second in order to be pleasing and loving, their love is often *defined* as putting themselves second in all things. They therefore limit themselves for another in a way that is not done for them.

We might even argue that women lose the gratitude one might gain for forsaking herself for others because in order to be properly selfless one must do it effortlessly, unquestioningly, almost invisibly. To do otherwise is to appear unloving.[32] In order to be canonized, a saint's miracles must be known and proven. Housework has often been described as invisible; it is so in part because it is supposed to be invisible. Whereas people (especially men) with jobs outside the home are expected to come home looking as though they had done a day's work, women who are homemakers are supposed to mask their labor by looking fresh and pleasing when their husbands come home. Of course, if their husbands' workday ends before dinner, the woman has not yet finished hers. Women are generally expected to cook the bacon even when they share the job of bringing it home. The distinction between a homemaker and an employed married woman is *not* whether she does the domestic labor or not. The distinction rests on whether she also works for pay. Thus, by marriage as it tends to be arranged, women both limit and devalue themselves.

Men gain a certain amount of freedom by having others to care for them, but they also lose the ability to be self-sufficient. Some theorists, primarily from the psychoanalytic tradition, go further than this in their assessment of the effects of male dependence upon women's self-sacrificing nurturance on men. Nancy Chodorow, for one, speculates that the process of developing a healthy independence from the mother in particular and women in general is hampered by the continuing dependence upon maternal duties and affections (even when these are administered by someone other than the mother).[33] This can lead to a continuing need to prove independence from and self-assertion over women, and a fear of female dominance. Although there is a degree to which we could argue that men have cared for themselves much more than they should, we can say that they have done this to a large degree by placing most of the burdens of care-giving on women. That burden will have to be shifted.

A final question, but the first for feminists, is who will care for the women? One answer is that with increased choice and freedom women will be more capable of caring for themselves. Feminist theorists have been arguing for at least two centuries that by locking women into dependence upon men and making their goals in life the service of others to the neglect of themselves, women have had great difficulty indeed in helping themselves.[34] It is curious that many of the people who are most keenly supportive of the idea of individual achievement and self-reliance are most opposed to removing the burdens that keep women from these ends.[35] Women must be allowed full participation in the governance of their lives both through "private" institutions such as the family and through the public and formal decision-making institutions of government.

But to say that women must care for themselves is not enough; there, too, we must argue that the entire community, including men, must care for them more as well. Until recently women have received only conditional care and only from husbands if they were married. Even financial upkeep, supposedly the obligation of the husband, depended solely on what the husband chose to give, as judicial precedent shows. Women treated to the violence of rape or battery at the hands of their husbands had little or no recourse. For too many women, the care offered by husbands has been a dubious blessing. As for care by the political system, even now there are those who wish to protect women by "not interfering" with family violence, to protect mothers struggling to raise their children by withdrawing as much public support as possible, and to protect young women and girls by keeping them from education about their emotions and bodies and then denying them access to abortion. There are even those who would protect human life by forcing women to carry to full term and nurture the result of a crime committed against them: rape.

The underlying theme of this book has been the relationship between public and private life and activity. This relationship may work in two ways. One realm may restrict the development of the other. By trying to enforce a radical juncture between the two we have, in effect, led the two to be mutually restrictive. We now understand the potential power of government too well to be able to tell ourselves that government can stay out of private life. What, for example, can we mean by saying the government should not "meddle" in family affairs? It can mean that we ask our representatives to turn their faces away from family relations which amount to the right of the strongest which, in turn, is hardly a norm supportive of democratic ideals.[36] The bifurcation of the public and private domains of life is based on a division of labor that restricts both sexes. These restrictions are not symmetrical, however; men occupy many more of the positions from which it is possible to determine which restrictions will be placed on whom.

The two domains may be related in such a way as to enrich and protect the other. Through the political system the right of the strongest can be overturned. The democratic theorists were not fuzzy-headed idealists when they argued that politics is an educational experience that extends deep into our private lives. Likewise, it is difficult to believe that politics and government are as democratic as they can be when people learn their values in a private life that is, in so many respects, inegalitarian and which restricts so many people from becoming integrated into political life.

Women, as we have seen, are considerably more a part of politics and government than they were in the past. Their private roles have only moderate, sometimes marginal effects on their political attitudes and behavior at the mass level. As we look to higher reaches of politics, however, we see increasing restrictions; governance is left more and more to men. The political liberation of women, their freedom to take full part in the governance of their lives, will depend on and require restructuring and re-evaluation of women's lives, men's lives, and the life of the community. The political community will have to become more committed to the development and fulfillment of human beings in order for integration to occur. This is not so, as many have argued, because women are more nurturant than men and will bring this sacred value with them into the public realm. Rather, the community as a whole will have to take responsibility for its members because that is the only way for a liberated society to survive once the private servants of public men have vanished. If we were to create this era of responsibility we might note, with Charlotte Perkins Gilman, "The big difference was that whereas our children grew up in private homes and families, with every effort made to protect and seclude them from a dangerous world, here they grew up in a wide, friendly world, and knew it was theirs, from the first."[37]

NOTES

1. Sidney Verba, Norman H. Nie, and Jae-on Kim, *Participation and Political Equality: A Seven Nation Comparison* (Cambridge: Cambridge University Press, 1978), p. 10.
2. Carole Pateman, *Participation and Democratic Theory* (New York: Cambridge University Press, 1970).
3. *Ibid.*, p. 104.
4. *Ibid.*, p. 105.
5. See especially Gabriel Almond and Sidney Verba, *The Civic Culture* (Boston: Little, Brown, 1965); Verba, Nie, and Kim, *Participation and Political Equality.*
6. It might appear that the conclusion is overdrawing the impediments women's roles pose against integration. This is not the case; the point throughout is that women's adult roles are impediments (especially given the relative insensitivity of these measures) but not the most important determinants of political roles at the mass level. To the degree that women's private roles affect the extent of their citizenship, we must look at the ways in which public policies shape their private roles.
7. Suzanne Britt Jordan, "My Turn: Married is Better," *Newsweek* (11 June 1979), 27. A number of researchers have demonstrated the ways in which the mass media both reflect gender role norms and serve as agents of gender role socialization. See, for example, Gaye Tuchman, Arlene Kaplan Daniels, and James Benet, eds., *Hearth and Home: Images of Women in the Mass Media* (New York: Oxford University Press, 1978).
8. There are now quite a few very good resources on women and the law. See Barbara Brown, Ann Freedman, Harriet Katz, and Alice Price, *Women's Rights and the Law: The Impact of the ERA on State Laws* (New York: Praeger, 1977); Leslie Friedman Goldstein, *The Con-*

stitutional Rights of Women: Cases in Law and Social Change (New York: Longman, 1979); Albie Sachs and Joan Hoff Wilson, *Sexism and the Law: Male Beliefs and Legal Bias* (New York: Free Press, 1979); and any issue of the *Women's Rights Law Reporter*.

9. See Jane Roberts Chapman and Margaret Gates, eds., *The Victimization of Women* (Beverly Hills: Sage, 1978).

10. Jane Roberts Chapman and Margaret Gates, eds., *Women into Wives: The Legal and Economic Impact of Marriage* (Beverly Hills: Sage, 1977), p. 36.

11. *Eisenstadt* v. *Baird* (1972) 405 U.S. 438.

12. *Roe* v. *Wade* (1973) 410 U.S. 113 and *Doe* v. *Bolton* (1973) 410 U.S. 179.

13. *Maher* v. *Roe* (1977) 97 S.Ct. 2376.

14. Chapman and Gates, *Women into Wives,* p. 307.

15. In Wisconsin, for example, a 1972 study showed that 44 percent of families receiving AFDC needed assistance because court-ordered child support payments were not being made. Governor's Commission on the Status of Women, *Wisconsin Women and the Law* (Madison: Governor's Commission, 1977), p. 12.

16. Rosalyn F. Baxandall, "Who Shall Care for Our Children? The History and Development of Day Care in the United States," in J. Freeman, ed., *Women: A Feminist Perspective* (Palo Alto: Mayfield, 1979), pp. 134–52.

17. For a review of the time use studies see John P. Robinson, "Household Technology and Household Work," in Sarah Fenstermaker Berk, ed., *Women and Household Labor* (Beverly Hills: Sage, 1980), pp. 29-52.

18. Walker, "Time Used by Husbands"; Angrist, Lave, and Mickelson, "How Working Mothers Manage."

19. Myra Marx Feree, "Working Class Feminism: A Consideration of the Consequences of Employment," *Sociological Quarterly* (Spring, 1980), 173-84.

20. On the history of and distinctions among "nondiscrimination" and "affirmative action," see California Commission on the Status of Women, *Impact ERA: Limitations and Possibilities* (Millbrae, Calif.: Les Femmes Publishing, 1976), and Norma K. Raffel, "Federal Laws and Regulations Prohibiting Sex Discrimination," in E. Snyder, ed., *The Study of Women: Enlarging Perspectives of Social Reality* (New York: Harper and Row, 1979), pp. 103-23.

21. Jean Bethke Elshtain, "Moral Woman and Immoral Man: A Consideration of the Public-Private Split and Its Political Ramifications," *Politics and Society* 4 (Winter, 1974), 453-74.

22. M. Kent Jennings, "Another Look at the Life Cycle and Political Participation," *American Journal of Political Science* 23 (Nov., 1979), 755-71; Virginia Sapiro, "Private Costs of Public Commitments or Public Commitments: Family Roles versus Political Ambition," *American Journal of Political Science* 26 (May, 1982), 265-79.

23. Harry Finkelstein, "Fathering and Marital Separation," in Dorothy McGuigan, ed., *New Research on Women and Sex Roles* (Ann Arbor: CEW, 1976), pp. 272-80.
24. Harry F. Keshet and Kristine M. Rosenthal, "Fathering after Marital Separation," *Social Work* 23 (Jan., 1978), 11-18.
25. For an extraordinary discussion of the power of male images, see Hélène Cixous, "The Laugh of the Medusa," *Signs* 1 (Summer, 1976), 875-94. In a most powerful discussion of the devastating effects of male images not just on women but on men as well, she argues that the Sirens, generally presented as beautiful women who sang enchanting songs and thereby drove sailors to crash to their deaths on the shores, were not really women but were men. Men created the myth and image of the dangerous and alluring Sirens, therefore it was a figment of men's imaginations (or, in real life, the results of male creation of women) that drove them to their own violent deaths.
26. Richard Sennett, *The Fall of Public Man* (New York: Random House, 1976); Robert Paul Wolff, "There's Nobody Here but Us Persons," in C. Gould and M. Wartofsky, eds., *Women and Philosophy* (New York: G.P. Putnam's Sons, 1976), pp. 128-44; Eli Zaretsky, *Capitalism, the Family, and Personal Life* (New York: Harper and Row, 1976).
27. Wolff, "There's Nobody Here but Us Persons," p. 133.
28. The contemporary experience of women in the Soviet Union serves as a good example. Some might argue that Soviet women have been brought into the public sphere because they constitute a majority of the workforce. The private sphere has not been integrated; women still do virtually all the household chores. Partly because women are still thought of in their traditional roles they remain segregated primarily in "female" jobs and are in no sense fully integrated into politics. See Dorothy Atkinson, Alexander Dallin, and Gail Warshovsky Lapidus, eds., *Women in Russia* (Stanford: Stanford University Press, 1977) and Lotta Lennon, "Women in the U.S.S.R.," *Problems of Communism* 20 (July-Aug., 1970), 47-58.
29. Pateman, *Participation and Democratic Theory*, p. 110.
30. For example, see Carol B. Stack, *All Our Kin: Strategies for Survival in a Black Community* (New York: Harper and Row, 1974).
31. By humanizing I mean both for the care giver and the care receiver. By suggestion in Nancy Chodorow, *The Reproduction of Mothering: Psychoanalysis and the Sociology of Gender* (Berkeley: University of California Press, 1978).
32. On women, love, and servility, see Thomas E. Hill, "Servility and Self-Respect," *The Monist* 57 (Jan., 1973), 87-104; Judith Tormey, "Exploitation, Oppression, and Self-Sacrifice," in Gould and Wartofsky, eds., *Women and Philosophy*, pp. 206-21; and Larry Blum, Marcia Homiak, Judy Housman, and Naomi Scheman, "Altruism and Women's Oppression," in Gould and Wartofsky, eds., *Women and Philosophy*, pp. 222-47.

33. Chodorow, *The Reproduction of Mothering.* See also Helen B. Andelin, *Fascinating Womanhood* (New York: Bantam, 1974), a conservative and fundamentalist who defends female playacting at submissiveness on the grounds that men are essentially children and need this kind of treatment.

34. For example, Mary Wollstonecraft, *A Vindication of the Rights of Women* (Baltimore: Penguin, 1975), first published in 1792.

35. For a discussion of women and self-reliance written by a member of the eminent group of defenders of this value in America, the Transcendentalists, see Margaret Fuller, "The Great Lawsuit. Man versus Men. Woman versus Women," in A. Rossi, ed., *The Feminist Papers* (New York: Bantam, 1974), pp. 158-82. First published in 1843.

36. For an early discussion of the contradictions between a private life based on the right of the strongest and democracy, see John Stuart Mill, "The Subjection of Women," in A. Rossi, ed., *Essays in Sex Equality* (Chicago: University of Chicago Press, 1970), pp. 125-242.

37. Charlotte Perkins Gilman, *Herland* (New York: Pantheon, 1979), p. 101. First published in 1898.

Bibliographic Essay

This book is intended not only for political scientists who focus their work specifically on the study of women, but also for those interested in political psychology and sociology who may be relatively unfamiliar with the literature on women and those interested in women's studies who are relatively unfamiliar with the literature on political behavior. What follows is an outline of some of the major works in the areas touched on in this book. More specific works are included in the notes.

For work on mass political behavior and attitudes, see Angus Campbell, Philip E. Converse, Warren E. Miller, and Donald E. Stokes, *The American Voter* (New York: Wiley, 1964); Sidney Verba and Norman Nie, *Participation in America: Political Democracy and Social Equality* (New York: Harper and Row, 1972); Norman Nie, Sidney Verba, and John Petrocik, *The Changing American Voter* (Cambridge: Harvard University Press, 1976); and W. Lance Bennett, *Public Opinion in American Politics* (New York: Harcourt, Brace, Jovanovich, 1980). For more theoretical work, see also Carole Pateman, *Participation and Democratic Theory* (New York: Cambridge University Press, 1970). An excellent comparative study, which builds on earlier work, is Sidney Verba, Norman Nie, and Jae-on Kim, *Participation and Political Equality: A Seven Nation Comparison* (New York: Cambridge University Press, 1978).

For political socialization, see M. Kent Jennings and Richard G. Niemi, *The Political Character of Adolescence* (Princeton: Princeton University Press, 1974) and, by the same authors, *Generations and Politics* (Princeton: Princeton University Press, 1981). These are the primary studies based on the data analyzed in this book. See also Stanley Renshon, ed., *Handbook of Political Socialization* (New York: Macmillan, 1977). On gender socialization, see Eleanor Maccoby, ed., *The Development of Sex Differences* (Stanford: Stanford University Press, 1966), and Lenore J. Weitzman, *Sex Role Socialization* (Palo Alto: Mayfield, 1979).

For works on the study of women and society see Diana Leonard Barker and Sheila Allen, eds., *Dependence and Exploitation in Work and Marriage* (New York: Longman, 1976); Harriet Holter, *Sex Roles and Social Structure* (Oslo: Universitetsforlaget, 1970); Jo Freeman, ed., *Women: A Feminist Perspective* (Palo Alto: Mayfield, 1979); Rayna Reiter, ed., *Toward an Anthropology of Women* (New York: Monthly Review Press, 1975); Michelle Zimbalist Rosaldo and Louise Lamphere, eds., *Women, Culture, and Society* (Stanford: Stanford University Press, 1974); Irene Frieze et al., eds., *Women and Sex Roles: A Social Psychological Perspective* (New York: Norton, 1978); and Zillah R. Eisenstein, ed., *Capitalist Patriarchy and the Case for Socialist Feminism* (New York: Monthly Review Press, 1979).

On women and mass political behavior and attitudes see Sara Evans, *Personal Politics: The Roots of Women's Liberation in the Civil Rights Movement and the New Left* (New York: Vintage, 1979); Claire Fulenwider, *Feminism in American Politics: A Study of Ideological Influence* (New York: Praeger, 1980); Marianne Githens and Jewel Prestage, eds., *A Portrait of Marginality: The Political Behavior of the American Woman* (New York: Longman, 1977); Jane Jaquette, ed., *Women in Politics* (New York: Wiley, 1974). See also Susan Moller Okin, *Women in Western Political Thought* (Princeton: Princeton University Press, 1979).

Although public policy on the status of women was only a subsidiary theme here, it is worth noting some of the highlights of this growing field. The Sage Yearbooks in Women's Policy Studies are particularly helpful; see Jane Roberts Chapman, ed., *Economic Independence for Women: The Foundation for Equal Rights* (Beverly Hills: Sage, 1976); Jane Roberts Chapman and Margaret Gates, eds., *Women into Wives: The Legal and Economic Impact of Marriage* (Beverly Hills: Sage, 1977); Jane Roberts Chapman and Margaret Gates, eds., *The Victimization of Women* (Beverly Hills: Sage, 1978); Karen Wolk Feinstein, ed., *Working Women and Families* (Beverly Hills: Sage, 1979); and Sara Fenstermaker Berk, ed., *Women and Household Labor* (Beverly Hills: Sage, 1980). See also Carolyn Teich Adams and Kathryn Teich Winston, *Mothers at Work: Public Policies in the United States, Sweden, and China* (New York: Longman, 1980) and Jo Freeman, *The Politics of Women's Liberation* (New York: Longman, 1974).

Finally, for discussion of how and why feminist scholars think differently from other scholars, see Carol Gould and Marx Wartofsky, eds., *Women and Philosophy* (New York: G.P. Putnam's Sons, 1976); Viola Klein, *The Feminine Character: History of an Ideology* (Urbana: University of Illinois Press, 1972); Julia A. Sherman and Evelyn T. Beck, eds., *The Prism of Sex: Essays in the Sociology of Knowledge* (Madison: University of

Wisconsin Press, 1979); Mary Vetterling-Braggin et al., eds., *Feminism and Philosophy* (Totowa: Littlefield, Adams, 1977) and Adrienne Rich, *On Lies, Secrets, and Silence* (New York: Norton, 1979).

Index

A Note on the Author

Virginia Sapiro is Associate Professor of Political Science and Women's Studies at the University of Wisconsin-Madison. She is the author or co-author of many articles and professional papers on women and politics including two that received awards for scholarly merit.